Special Thanks to:

Alban Barré, Patrice Hamel, Stephan May, Pascal Launay, Mélodie, Cinemalta, Patrick Luthi, Young-sook Kim, Antoine Moreau, Yunjeong Kim, Ina Park, Cineclick Asia, James Velaise, Pretty Pictures, Angela Detanico, Rafael Lain, Magali Guyon
and
Solal Guyon-Barré

Edité avec le concours du Ministère Français chargé de la Culture - Centre National du Livre (aide à la traduction).

For the translation published with the help of the Ministère Français chargé de la Culture - Centre National du Livre.

1 cité Riverin
750010 Paris
http://www.disvoir.com

ISBN : 2-914563-21-3
PRINTED IN EUROPE

KIM KI DUK

THIS SERIES EDITED BY DANIÈLE RIVIÈRE

In the same series

TSAI MING LIANG
Jean-Pierre Rhem
Olivier Joyard
Danièle Rivière

BRUNO DUMONT
Sebastien Ors
Philippe Tancelin
Valérie Jouve

WONG KAR WAI
Jean-Marc Lalanne
David Martinez
Ackbar Abbas
Jimmy Ngai

ATOM EGOYAN
Carole Desbarats
Jacinto Lageira
Danièle Rivière
Paul Virilio

PETER GREENAWAY
Daniel Caux
Michel Field
Florence de Mèredieu
Philippe Pilard
Michael Nyman

RAOUL RUIZ
Christine Buci-Glucksmann
Fabrice Revault D'Allonnes

MANOEL DE OLIVEIRA
Yann Lardeau
Philippe Tancelin
Jacques Parsi

KIM KI DUK

ADRIEN GOMBEAUD

ANAÏD DEMIR

CÉDRIC LAGANDRÉ

CATHERINE CAPDEVILLE-ZENG

DANIELE RIVIERE

Translated from the French by PAUL BUCK & CATHERINE PETIT

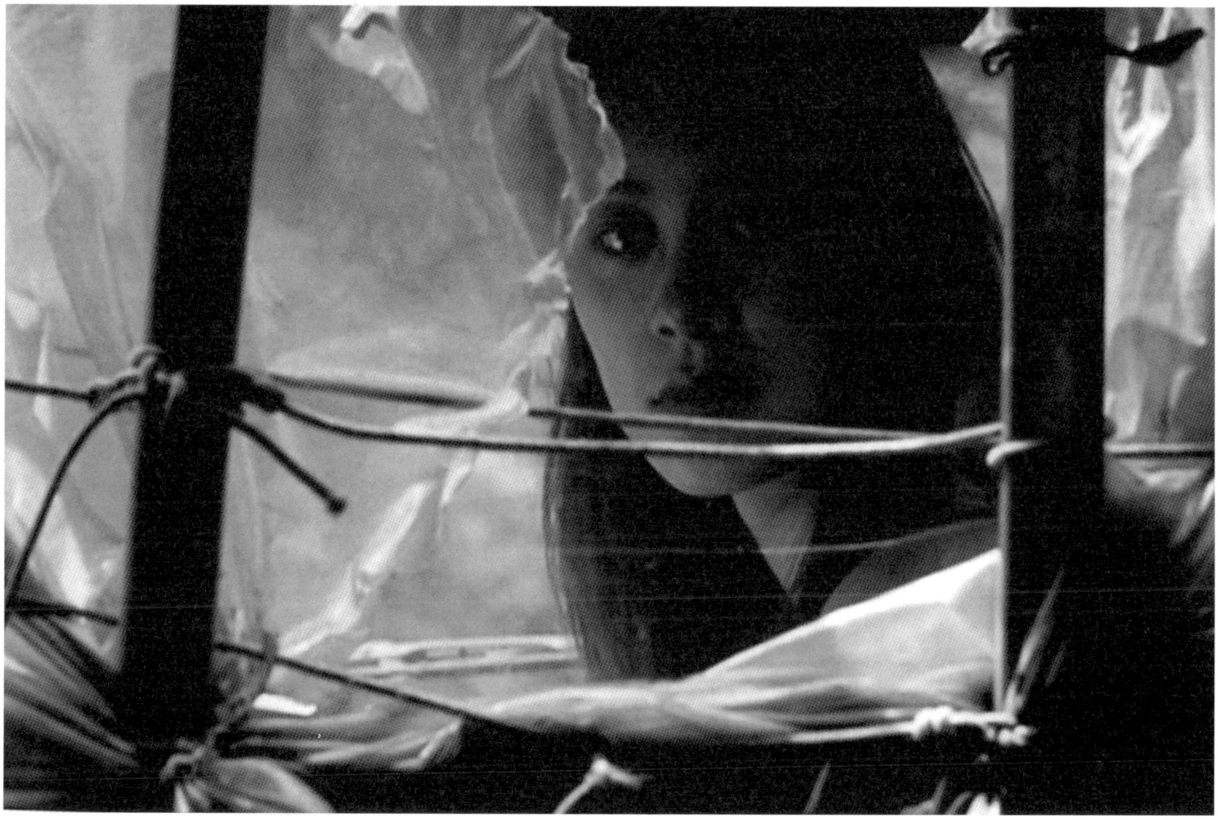

◀ 1

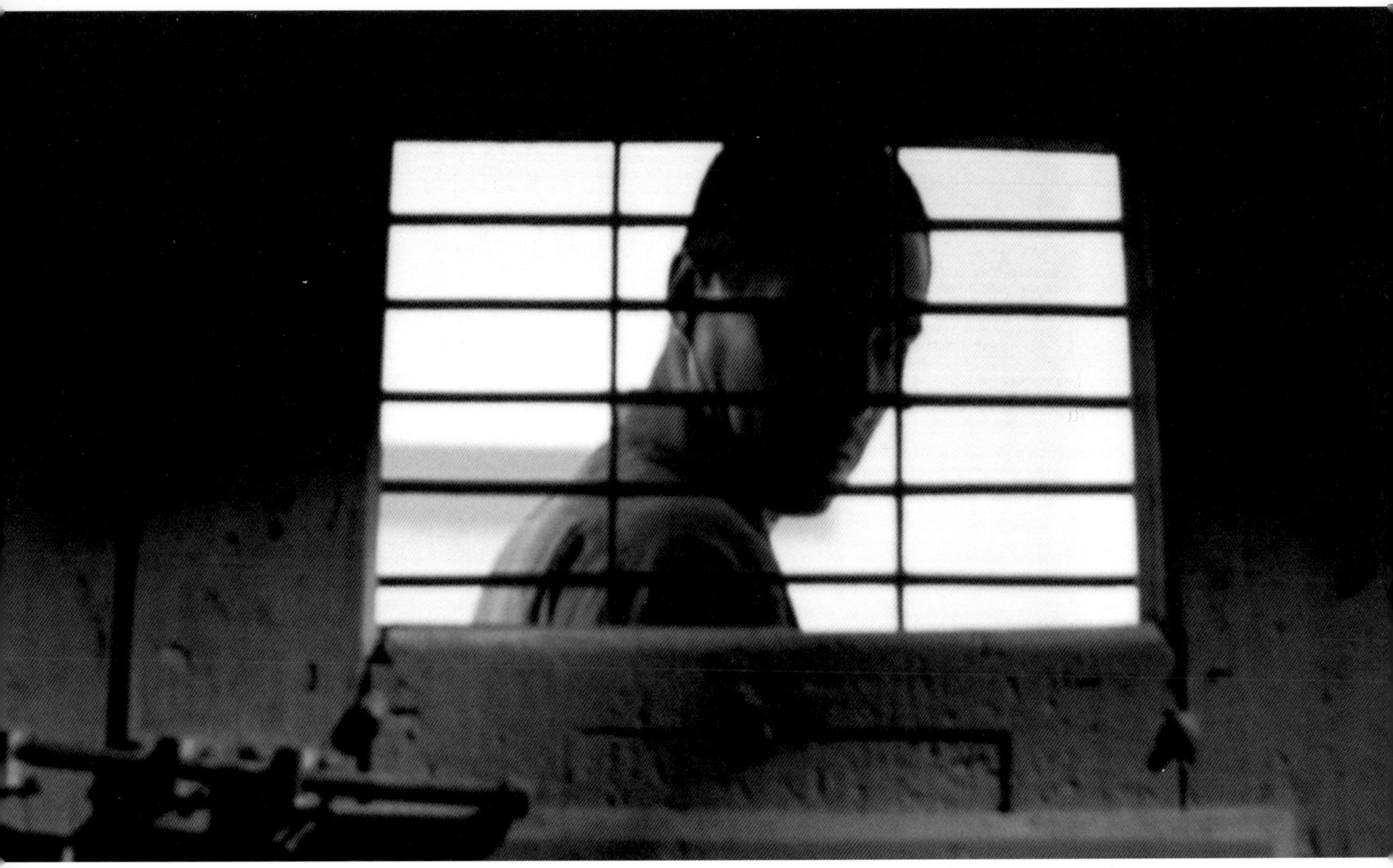

2 ▲

BREAK ON THROUGH

I found an island in your arms
Country in your eyes
Arms that chain us
Eyes that lie
Break on through to the other side

(Break on through - The Doors)

At the beginning of *Bad Guy*, a girl is chatting with her boyfriend. She smiles, shifts from one foot to the other, touches his cheek with her hand, making him smile. He has a neat fringe and the doe-eyes of the perfect student. They are the sign of a good match for the future. Suddenly, a lout appears with hungry wolf eyes. He grabs the teenage girl, forces her to turn around and violently presses his mouth against hers. It's not a kiss, it's a bite. She struggles, the dashing boyfriend tries to separate them, hits the intruder with a metal trash can. Nothing works. The man is glued to the girl, planted on her. Soldiers intervene and beat him up. The girl, disgusted, spits in her attacker's face. Nothing will part them now.

The idea of sudden appearance is a familiar pattern in Kim Ki-duk's cinema, though those brutal beginnings more generally act as the signature of the Nineties generation. Several films from that period start with that type of explosion. Those openings, like blasts of air, correspond to the sudden arrival at the forefront of the young bucks of Korean cinema. The second half of the Nineties was undoubtedly the most intense period Korean cinema has ever known. Kim Ki-duk started in 1996, at the age of thirty-four, with *Crocodile*. That same year, Hong Sang-soo also shot his first film, *The Day a Pig Fell Into the Well*, and Lee Chang-dong was preparing *Green Fish*, which was made in 1997. In 1998, Kim Ji-woon's *The Quiet Family* came out, as well as Im Sang-soo's *Girls' night out*. With no particular specialized training, they would all become active and important film directors[1]. The reconstruction of Korean cinema followed the process of democratization. Dictatorship officially ended in 1993 with the election of Kim Young-sam. After twenty years of a severe military regime, the old studios were rusted. The old generation of film directors had shaped their assistants to be like them, incapable thus of responding to the desires of a young audience whom they didn't understand. The new producers were open to fresh personalities coming from diverse horizons. Im Sang-soo had studied sociology, Lee Chang-dong was a writer, Kim Ji-woon a fringe-theatre director, Hong Sang-soo, just back

[1] Hong Sang-soo has since shot, among others, *Virgin Stripped Bare by Her Bachelors, Woman Is the Future of Man, A Tale of Cinema*... Lee Chang-dong has made, *Peppermint Candy* and *Oasis* before becoming Minister of Culture, then resigning in 2002. Kim Ji-woon has shot *A Tale of Two Sisters* and *A Bittersweet Life*. Im Sang-soo, notably, *The President's Last Bang*.

from Chicago, an eternal student. None however came from as far away as Kim Ki-duk. It appears that in the first part of his life, Kim Ki-duk accumulated all the experiences possible to re-inscribe them into his future cinema. By walking on the edge for thirty years, Kim Ki-duk physically explored the themes of his future cinema: wandering, escape and, above all, survival. Born in 1960 in a mountain village in the Kyongsang province, he studied agriculture and started work in a factory at the age of seventeen. He did a prolonged military service in the *marines*, then decided to become a priest and retreated into a Catholic monastery. He started painting. With little money, he travelled through Europe, from Finland to Greece. He finally settled near Montpellier, where he sold his paintings in the street, and where, he recalled, he saw three films: *Les Amants du Pont-Neuf*, *The Lover* and *The Silence of the Lambs*. He returned to Korea and sent two scripts to various competitions. One was called *Painter and Prisoner*, the second *Illegal Crossing*. Both won prizes in 1994. Neither were shot, but he succeeded in financing a third project, *Crocodile*, whose shooting started in 1996.

Kim Ki-duk's first films are logically enough marked by French aesthetics. *Crocodile* tells the story of a tramp and a girl under a bridge in Seoul and is largely inspired by Léos Carax's *Les Amants du Pont-Neuf* (which had been a very big commercial success in Korea, along with other Carax films). *Wild Animals*, his follow-up film, was set in Paris. In that film Kim Ki-duk directs Denis Lavant, one of the Carax regulars, as well as Richard Bohringer, playing a role similar to the one in *Diva*. However, those two first films were not a commercial success and he didn't know, when he wrote his next script, if the third opus would ever be made. The theme of survival caught up with him. He had to dig his teeth deeper into cinema if he didn't want to risk losing it.

Kim Ki-duk was again saved by a competition. The Kofic (Korean Film Commission) awarded a prize for the script of *Birdcage Inn*. Production could begin. The film finally gained some success. Water, animals, prostitution… Kim Ki-duk gave form to the same obsessions as in his previous films, in a *mise-en-scène* still much inspired by French cinema (the deserted beach being reminiscent of *Betty Blue*). However, marketing insisted on the scandalous side of the story in which a sensible student takes on the identity of a prostitute. In 1998, Korea was shaken too by Im Sang-soo's *Girls' night out*, in which a group of girlfriends share details of their sexual life, as well as by E J Yong's first film, *An Affair*, in which the hero falls in love with his future sister-in-law, much older than him. The audience obviously needed to be shocked. Kim Ki-duk came at the right time. The renaissance of Korean cinema was a national project, a kind of big building site. It was a matter of rebuilding a dying industry, reconciling the Korean people with their cinema and producing films capable of carrying forth the image of a nation at film festivals, for Korea was seeking to exist beyond factories for electronic components and cheap electric goods. The country launched a campaign to obtain a Nobel prize, and encouraged the film directors capable of having a dialogue with the Chinese or the Iranians at the big international film events. *Birdcage Inn* was invited to the Berlin, Karlovy Vary and Montreal festivals… Kim Ki-duk took on the role of champion, a role that he still assumes today. *The Isle*, his next film, preceded by a carefully orchestrated scandalous reputation, was presented in Venice, Rotterdam, and Toronto, and well distributed in the West. Above all, Kim Ki-duk's films are successes at International film festivals, cult objects abroad and curiosities in his own country. He has consolidated his status in South Korean cinema with that recipe: polemics in Korea, prizes abroad. He takes a personal short cut, away from the economic motorways of the cinema industry. As if to mark that freedom, he made *Real Fiction* (2000), an experimental project, a kind of flamboyant manifesto of a cinema in the making. The film was shot in a few hours. Kim Ki-duk had placed cameras around a district in Seoul and the film was shot like that, with one single take per scene, captured from various angles by an armada of objectives worthy of a super surveillance video camera system. The director looks like he is racing down a hill at full tilt, brandishing speed and improvisation like a banner. He sides radically with those extremists who, with André Breton, believe that "beauty will be convulsive or not". The other film, whose style is radically opposed, but which offers another key to the Kim Ki-duk method is *Spring, Summer, Fall, Winter... and Spring* (2003). It is not a film *about* Buddhism, but a buddhist film in substance as well as in form (he faithfully retakes the structure of *Why Did Bodhi Dharma Leave for the East?* which was the first success of Korean cinema abroad in 1989). The seasons pass in a monastery where a young monk lives his life. Each represents a step in a man's life. At the end, spring returns, at the same time similar to the previous one, and yet new, enriched by the previous seasons. That cycle is not closed on itself like a hoop, but takes the shape of an ascending spiral, in constant progression. *Spring, Summer, Fall, Winter… and Spring* is the only film in which Kim Ki-duk appears as an actor. It is a way to place himself personally in that time, to merge into that progression in convolutions. Though Kim Ki-duk is officially a protestant, his cinematic practise obviously follows Buddhist time and dynamics. All his characters are re-incarnations. United together, they form a long farandole dance coiled like a snake. They hold each other's hand, dragging each other along into a collective leaping and bounding. The American soldier hunted down by the villagers in *Address Unknown* becomes the mad captain in *Coast Guard* pursued by his own unit. To escape them, he

3 ▶

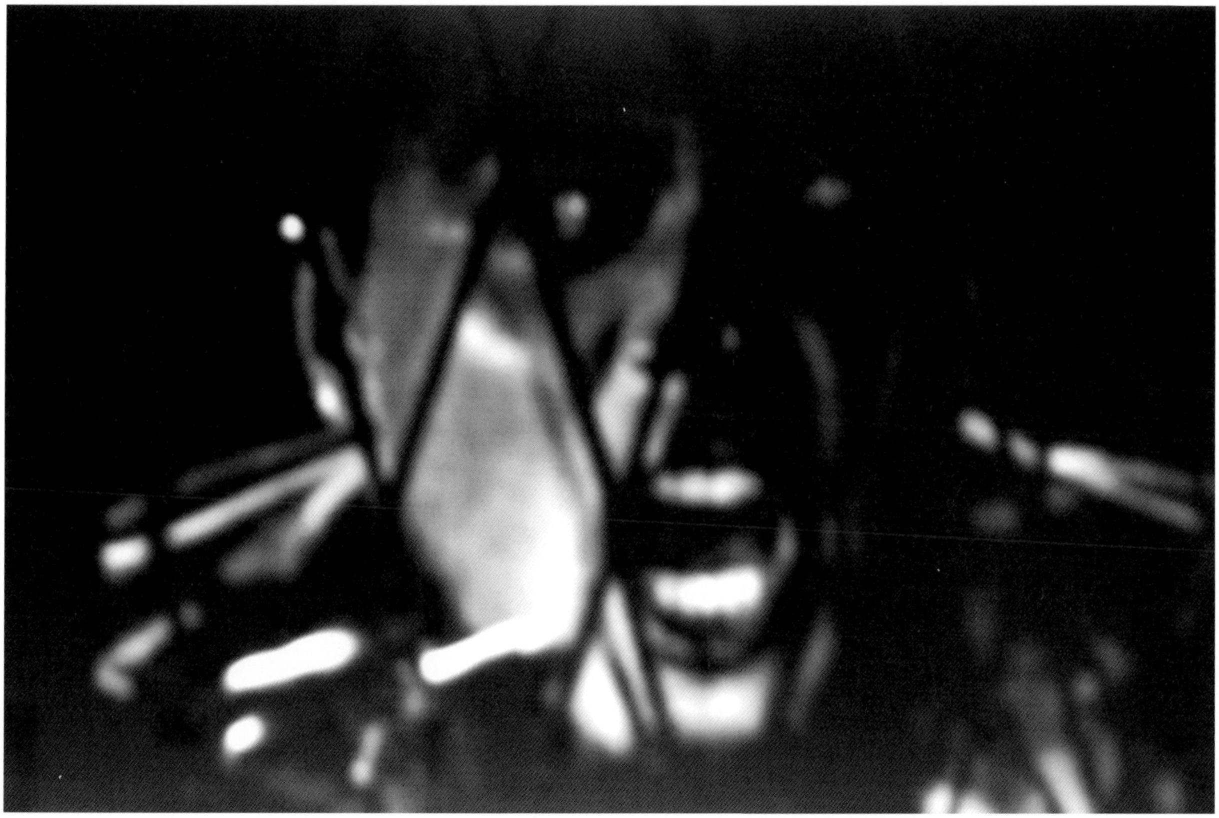

becomes a ghost, discreetly gliding along the sides through the barbed wire. He pre-figures the burglar in *3-iron,* who floats like a spectre, invisible, from house to house. In the same way, the two girls in *Samaritan Girl* are manifestations of the prostitute and the student who already swapped identities in *Birdcage Inn*... One understands then why Kim Ki-duk shoots so much and so fast. He needs to carry on at all costs making that frenetic farandole dance: one film invokes another, one character leads to the next in the same procession. Like the cycle of seasons, that movement cannot end. For ending is dying.

At the end of *Bad Guy*, the lout has turned the student into a prostitute. He has thrown an old mattress into the back of a van and sold the body of his beloved to the fishermen exhausted by a night at sea. Having made money from a few 'quickies', the couple drive off along the corniche road. The vehicle ventures into the distance. The screen turns to black. On the right, the vehicle has left its mark: a small scarlet red square stands out on the dark background... like a stain of indelible blood? Like an island in a dark ocean?

In *Wild Animals*, a painter throws blood on a canvas, as if to create a violent work from body fluids. The stain is the trace of a spontaneous gesture, a form dedicated to chance. Kim Ki-duk though works on his aesthetics. The colours he uses are harmonious or contrast with a certain degree of aggressiveness, the places are photogenic, the sets (sometimes designed by Kim himself) carefully constructed or chosen... But he feels the need to shoot in the space of a few days (*Spring, Summer, Fall, Winter... and Spring* remains an exception for it was shot over a year). Deliberately, he shoots in a few takes after just a few rehearsals. In other words, that sophistication must spring from a sudden gesture. Kim merely follows the psychology of the characters by connecting to the tradition of calligraphy.

Kim Ki-duk's heroes don't anticipate events. The most spontaneous being of course murder, mutilation or suicide. It seems that for Kim Ki-duk nothing is more beautiful than that moment when the body changes its normal working condition, no longer obeys the mind, tears itself away from the straight jacket of the spirit to react only to instinct, like a knee becoming taut after the sharp tap of a mallet. The director orchestrates a world which acts impulsively. On instincts of sex and death mainly. Thus, the characters in *The Isle* don't make a conscious decision to swallow fish-hooks or push them into a vagina. The bad guy doesn't decide to throw himself on the pretty and innocent student. The young country girl in *Address Unknown* doesn't take the decision to gouge out her eye. The schoolgirl in *Samaritan Girl* doesn't decide to jump through the motel window, no more than – later – her client thinks before he too throws himself through the window in front of his family.

They all spring forward, rushing instinctively towards the unknown and death, freed from all notions of good and bad, pain or pleasure. They are so determined that nothing, especially morality or danger, could stop them. Kim Ki-duk is not really interested in violence or sex, but in that rapid *crossing to the other side*, that moment when the impulse of the body sweeps over the forces of reason. When the man let himself be overwhelmed by his nature, the mask drops, he is back to his original state, he becomes again a "wild animal" but also a fragile, vulnerable, suffering being. In reaching that nakedness of feeling, he is at the same time more brutal and more human. Crime, the unavoidable result of that phenomenon, is then committed with a weapon of fortune, somehow incongruous: a frozen fish, a brick, a golf club, a secateurs, a piece of shattered glass... The golf ball in *3-iron* is the perfect symbol of that phenomenon. Tied to a tree, it is used by the amateur golfer and it returns to the tree after each practice swing... until the metal thread comes loose and the ball flies off, twists like a furious missile, whirling around to crash through a windscreen and kill an occupant.

Two characters are emblematic of that transformation for they both have a job linked to order: the soldier and the policeman. The policeman in *Samaritan Girl* discovers that his daughter is a prostitute. He is a pious and meticulous man. One can see it especially in the way he applies himself when he does the cooking, wakes up his daughter by delicately placing headphones over her ears which play an Erik Satie piece. Kim Ki-duk captures his transformation in the increase of his palpitating breathing. He literally lets himself go: his daughter notices that he no longer shaves, no longer washes. His stare is blank and he walks mechanically towards murder... He confronts one of his daughter's clients in the public lavatory of a park. He provokes him by urinating on him, beats him up with a pair of handcuffs, then finishes him off with a brick. The gesture is slow, mechanical, measured like the strokes of a clock. Each blow soils the clean, smooth and white tiled floor with big ochre splashes. Blood, ever present in Kim Ki-duk's films (as to a lesser extent are piss and shit), is nothing but the visual manifestation of that internal part of the body which re-appears in floods, that animality deep buried and bubbling, which spurts like a red scream. The Coast Guard's journey is more surprising still. The training of sailors is filmed almost like a ritual. They repeat the same movements in order to resist an invisible enemy, an invasion which never happens. But by constantly repeating those defence movements, the illusion that the enemy is about to attack becomes so real that it ends up happening. Then, in a perfectly co-ordinated mechanism, the coast guard machine-guns, then shells an innocent couple playing about on the beach. The young man is pulverized, the young girl seriously injured. At the end of the film, having gone mad, wandering in a street in Seoul, the soldier repeats

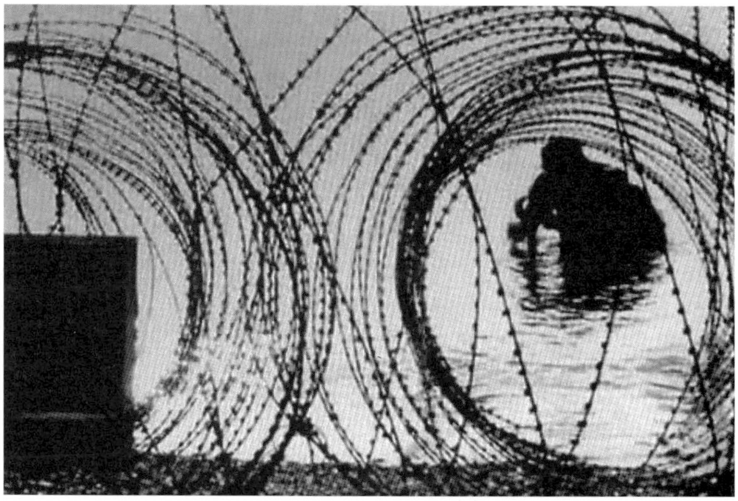

◀ 4

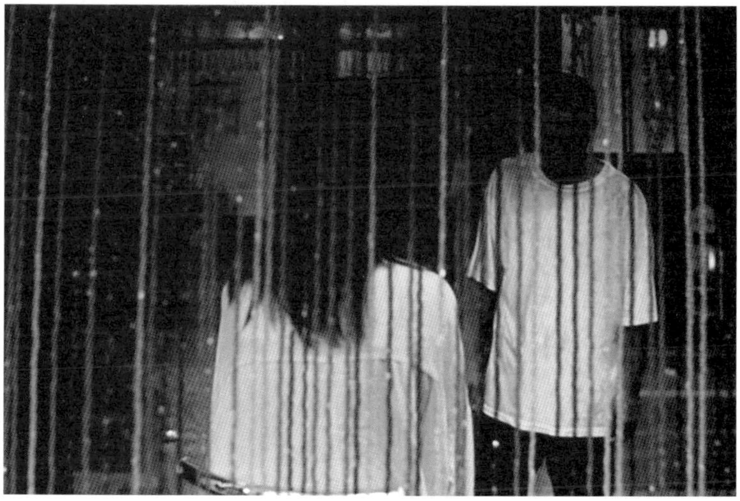

◀ 5

6 ▶

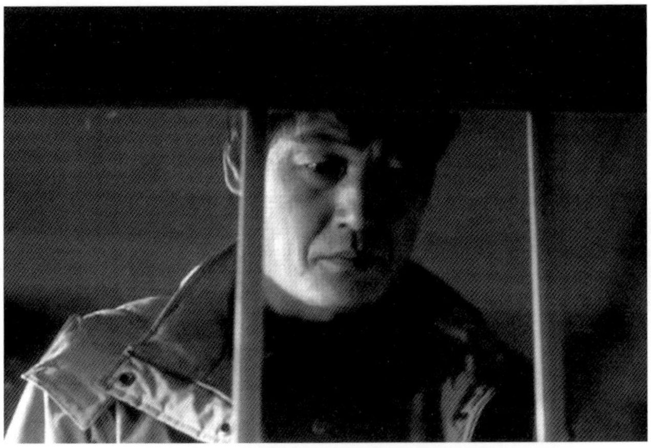

7 ▶

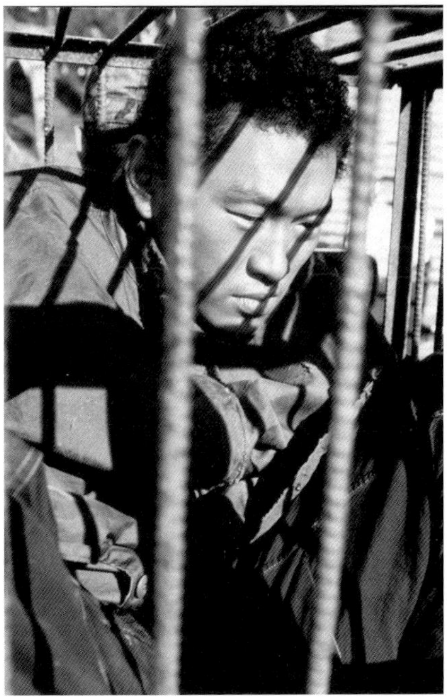

8 ▼

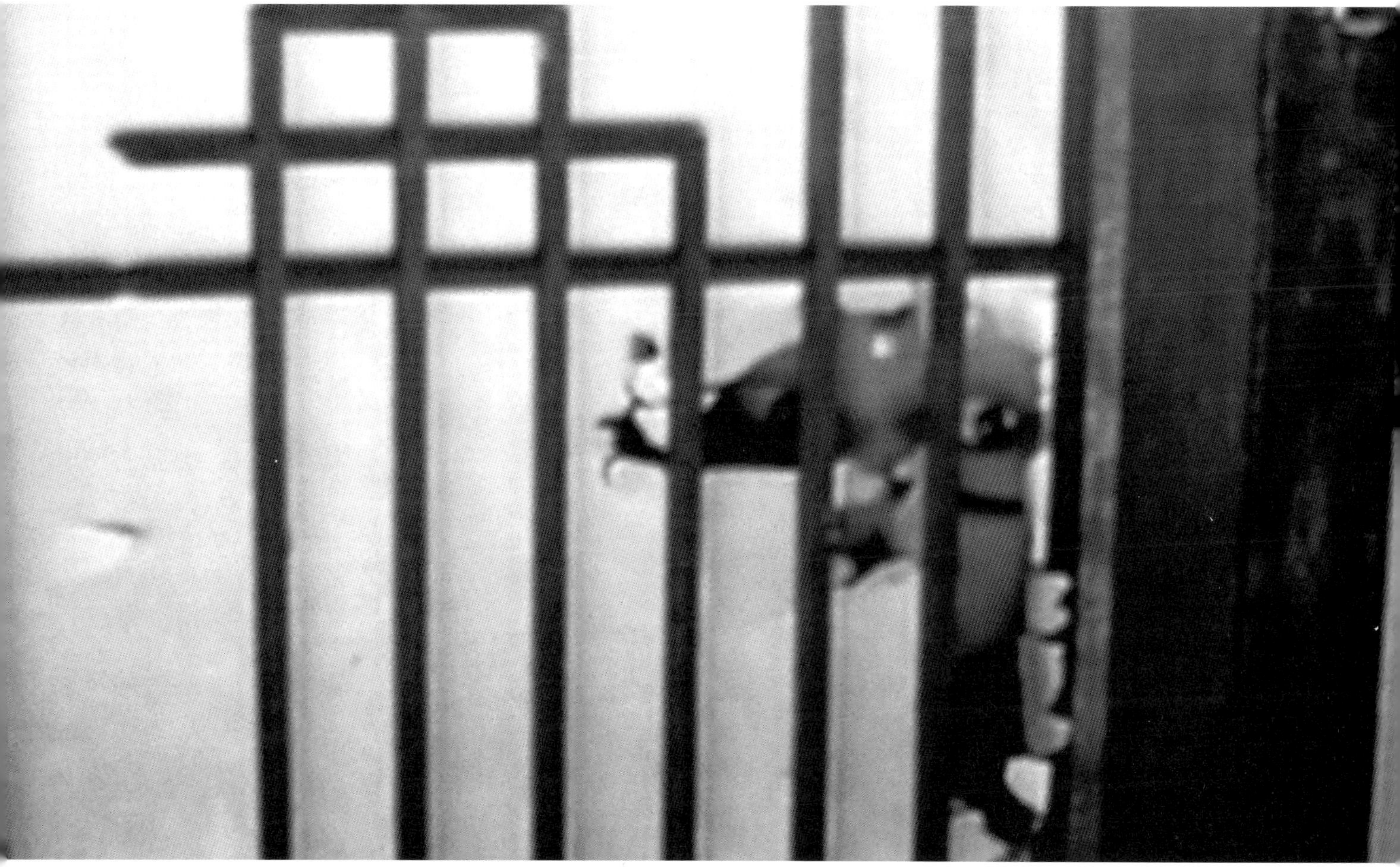

the combat movements with a bayonet. The passers-by crowd around him and enjoy the dance they take for a display. Those movements have no meaning for them. Then, coldly and brutally, the coast guard plunges his bayonet into one of the spectator's stomachs.

In that regard Kim Ki-duk is simply proposing a degenerate setting of a ritual and an idea quite widespread in the Far East: the ritual is useful because, by creating automatisms, it carries the action to its highest degree of effectiveness. The most unthinking gesture is the most operative. It is only acquired through repetition. Confucius says in his Conversations: "If his bearing is right, all will be accomplished without the need to give orders; if his bearing is not right, he will command but nobody will obey."[2] The master doesn't offer here a mere lesson in how to live. He implies the authority of the body over the mind. The body, its bearing, generates an impeccable and automatic order. That same idea is found in the Zhuang-zi: "That passage to a superior regime, that moment when a kind of shifting happens, when, to the movements artificially coordinated and controlled by consciousness is substituted suddenly a 'functioning of things' much more complete which, taking over, unloads the conscience of the biggest part of its tasks and abolishes efforts."[3] The most famous example is of course that of the butcher Ting. Zhuang-zi tells how the prince passes in front of a particularly skilful butcher and asks him the secret of his art. At the beginning of his career, the butcher saw the beef. After three years of practice, he only saw parts of the beef. Now he sees the beef in his mind, without seeing it with his eyes. His senses no longer intervene. His mind acts automatically and the blade inserts itself in the interstices of the carcass. The butcher Ting bones the beef perfectly, without ever using his knife, for he works without thinking about his movements, like one walks or chews one's food. The Coast Guard would then be the cursed child or the degenerate product of that philosophy, of that training and education. The army itself seems involved in terrible and well-oiled wheels, responding to the criminal act of the Coast Guard with a solemn and well-orchestrated ceremony. The victim, having escaped the carnage, and having become mad, is raped by the entire regiment with the same terrifying mechanism. The temptation of the border takes on here a political meaning in a country divided for more than fifty years. When she drags her boyfriend onto the beach to make love in the middle of a demilitarized zone, the border for her is only a game, an abstract convention one could break free from. But in reality the border is as absurd as it is real, whatever the violence of the consequences, for her as for all of Kim Ki-duk's heroes, there is no going back or stopping once the threshold has been crossed. The only solution, that of the Bad Guy and his "fiancee" for example, but also that of the schoolgirl in *Samaritan Girl* or the old sailor and the girl in *The Bow*, is to go to the end of the road towards which our instincts have pushed us. In *Spring,*

[2] Trad. Jean Lévi in *Confucius* Ed. Albin Michel Coll. Spiritualités Vivantes. 2003 p130.

[3] Jean François Billeter, *Leçons sur le Tchouang-Tseu* Ed. Allia.2002. p56.

Summer, Fall, Winter… and Spring, when the child tortures a frog or a fish by tying them to a pebble, the monk responds by weighting the boy with a stone: *"if any one of them dies you will carry the stone in your heart for as long as you live"*. By forcing him later to carve sutras in the wood of the temple, he doesn't show him anything else: each gesture is definitive, each spring is unique, each stain is indelible.

Seeing the painter in *Wild Animals* creating his curious blood work, one obviously thinks about Jackson Pollock and 'action painting'. I've already underlined the important influence of the West on the work of Kim Ki-duk. He confesses having been particularly interested in Western painting, and that this interest prompted him to travel and stay in Europe, especially in France. His approach however is more cross-mixed than it appears. The West discovered the value of improvisation quite late with jazz, for example, which had a considerable impact on Pollock and a film director like Cassavetes. Yet Pollock admitted himself that his method could be allied to more distant and ancient Asian practices. The energetic thick and thin strokes, the firm prints of his brush on the canvas also echo the works of the masters of "wild calligraphy".

We know, for example, that in the 8th century, the Chinese Zhang Xu used to write with his fingers or hair dipped in ink. The great calligraphers and painters of the Far East reached the quintessence of their art in moments of trance, when, aided by alcohol, their bodies took over their minds. The poet Su Dongpo (11th century) described a painter thus: *"When Yu-ko painted a bamboo, he no longer saw himself, and that's not saying a lot that he no longer saw himself; for, possessed, he left behind his own body; that body transformed, became bamboo, generating endless new blooms."*[4] In Im Kwon-taek's film *Chihwaseon* we see how the painter Owon wakes up in the morning completely astonished to discover in his studio the monstrously beautiful painting he has given birth to during his drunken night. Japanese artists from the *gutail* movement who painted with all parts of their body, leaving on the canvas or the paper traces of their passage, are as much the heirs of traditional calligraphy as the heirs of French informal art or, as has been often repeated, the precursors of Action Painting. Murakami Saburo's work *Passing Through* (1956) is, for example, a kind of monumental calligraphy. The artist has laid out a series of paper screens which he then goes through, running, leaving a precise trace of his passage through the sheets. Passing through is also, like the butcher Ting, "to change one's regime" and to create nothing more than the blurred trace of an impulse. Passing through or painted, the paper-screen captured every movement, even the most clumsy skidding. Contrary to the canvas of the Western painter, it allows no re-touching and permits no hesitation. The character is

[4] Trad. François Cheng, *Souffle Esprit* Ed. du Seuil, 1989 p76.

9 ▶

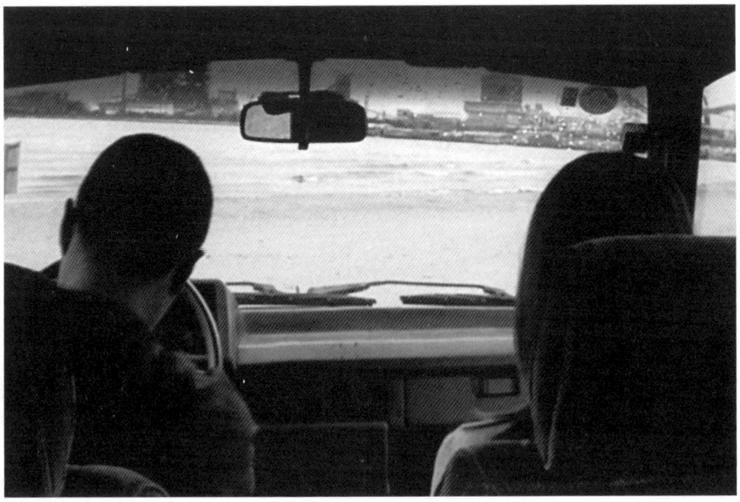

10 ▶

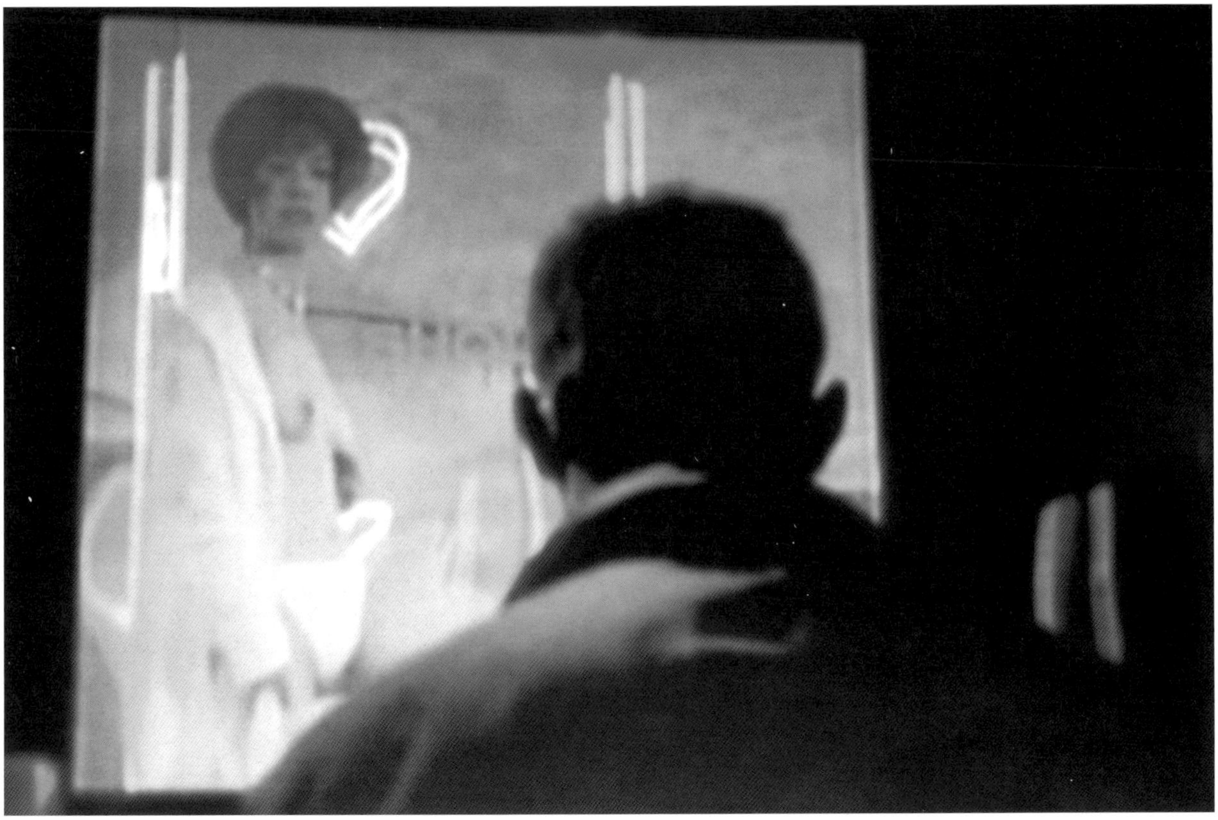

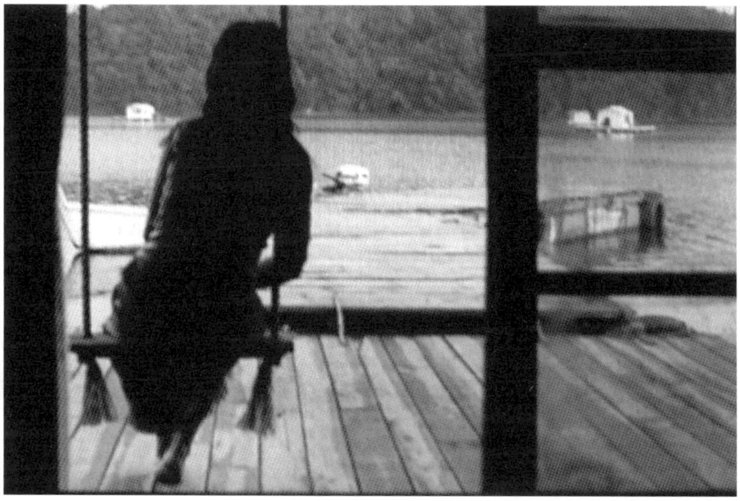

◀ 11

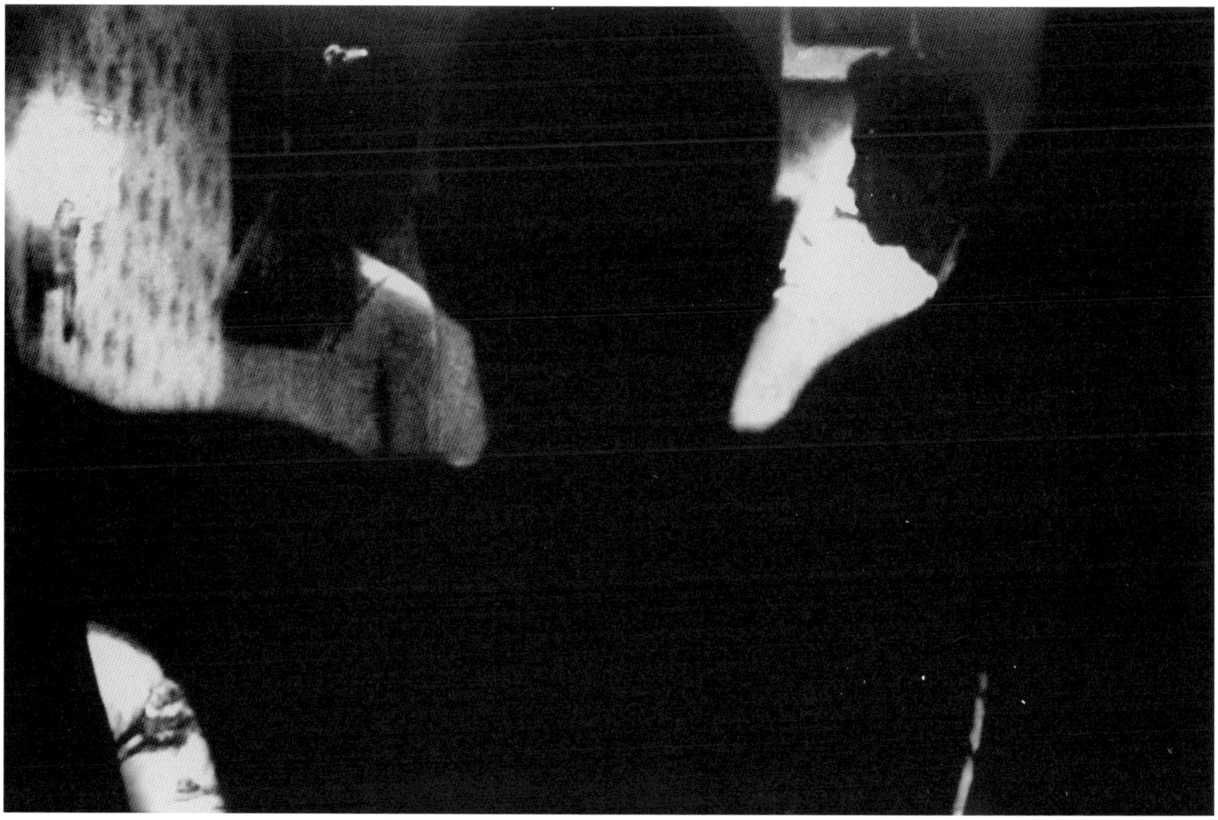

◀ 12

inscribed quickly with one gesture which involves the whole body. The sign is the trace of that movement and rhythm. The expert even says he can read in it the breathing of the artist. We are truly into the process of films shot in fifteen days, like *Samaritan Girl*, or in a few hours like *Real Fiction*. In those two films, Kim Ki-duk also shares his will to make of that visual art a performance or even a show. As the great calligraphers expressed themselves publicly on the walls or on the ground, he regularly shoots in the street. In *Samaritan Girl* and at the end of *Real Fiction*, the passers-by watching the shooting are visible in the background. Kim Ki-duk's cinema has sometimes sought the sophistication of studios, but he fits more suitably in the line of street artists. If he has often worked with more or less confirmed artists, he is only interested in those who express themselves freely: monks, tramps or penniless students. *Wild Animals* is the portrait, very autobiographical and inspired by his own stay in Europe, of that type of creative artist. In the street, painters meet acrobats, mimes and prostitutes, all of whom for Kim Ki-duk belong to the same universe. The very ironic ending to *Bad Guy* really resembles the beginning of a tale about a long poetic bohemian journey which would recount the destiny of two wandering artists. The street arts, whose beauty Kim Ki-duk sings about, share with calligraphy that preoccupation for spontaneousness.

In reality, throughout its history, Korea has shown more creativity in that type of creation and in artisinal craft than in the noble arts of the court. Though Kim Ki-duk wants, or wanted to experiment when he started, he shows himself increasingly to be the bearer of an artistic tradition that he cultivates more and more. Without ever having adapted a book, he comes straight from that literature which, since the 17th century, has circulated in the small lopsided bookstalls found in markets between pig's trotters and piles of cabbages. The street smells have seeped into the short texts, fed by the vigour of daily life. Today still, Korean literature prefers the form of short effective stories than the long novel; poetry remains a major genre in Korea. The *pansori*, an improvised traditional song, evoked by Im Kwon-taek in *Sopyeonjae* and in *Chunhyang* was also born on the road. Itinerant artists, at the same time singers and storytellers, sitting on a simple straw mat, improvise around a well-known story. Those performances can last as long as eight hours and are often acted until the artist's collapse from exhaustion. There is again here that "change of regime", when the singer goes from one character to another, when he forgets his text to throw himself, like a jazz saxophonist, into an improvised cavalcade. About Kim Ki-duk one could also evoke those street tumblers who used to perform on village squares, poking fun at the powerful during insolent shows, while deliberately searching for still more instability. Kim Ki-duk, in his cinematic practice itself, has been fed on that popular Korean cultural background.

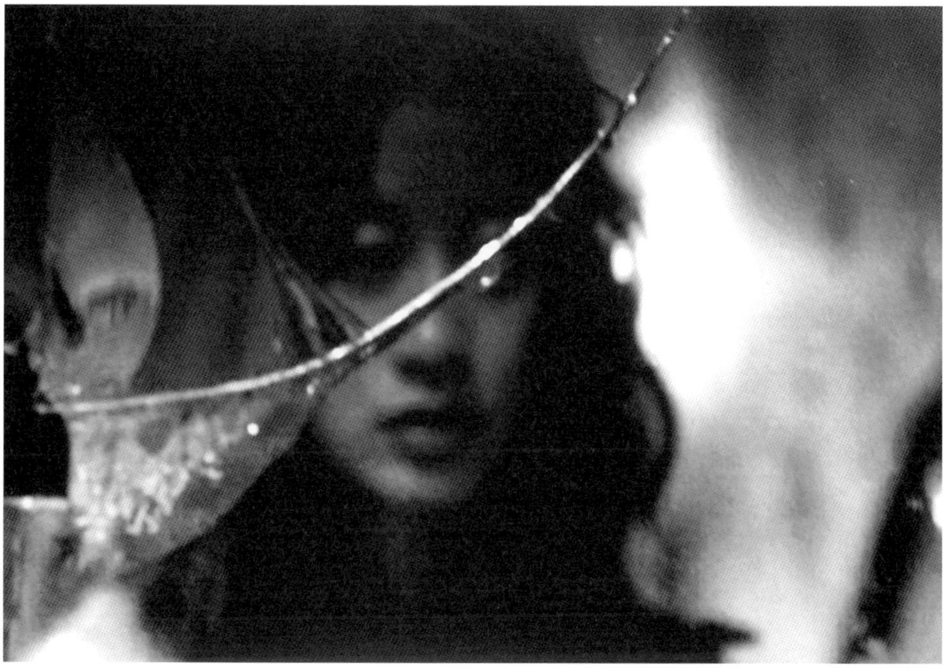

◀ 13

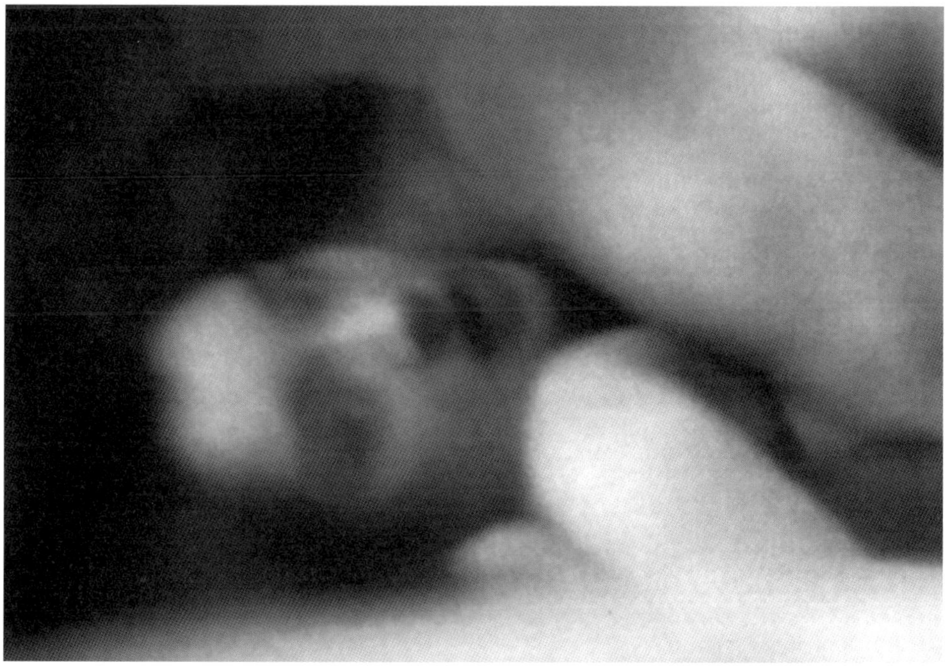

◀ 14

More than oil painting, which he admired and wanted to practice, he discovered during his travels through Europe a love for portraits in charcoal, a taste for those ephemeral drawings sold for a few coins straight after their execution.

In the role of the monk, Kim Ki-duk sketches the portrait of the child in *Spring, Summer, Fall, Winter… and Spring*. Those anonymous works of art have the virtue of reducing faces to a few essential strokes. It is the way Kim Ki-duk handles one by one the "clients" in *Samaritan Girl*, who only appear for a few seconds in one or two scenes. Their individuality rapidly stands out like shadows on the canson paper, a surplus of black roughly spread with one movement of the hand or a finger moistened with saliva. Those pictures circulate freely, escaping the hammer of the auctioneer as one escapes the truncheon of a cop. Preferring the forecourt of Beaubourg to the galleries of the Louvre, Kim Ki-duk has found in the Westen world a reflection on what the Far East used to contain (and Korea doubtlessly more than any other country): a form of vivid, brutal and corporeal beauty. "*The final aim of the acrobat-calligrapher is to dazzle. To move is the aim of the artist calligrapher. The latter has a more difficult role still than that of the actor, for he cannot nor should he prepare his role through rehearsals. It's true that he trains daily. But as Dong Qichang said: one has to acquire dexterity first, then to rediscover naivety and clumsiness.*"[5] The numerous prizes that Kim Ki-duk has been fortunate enough to collect in festivals over these last few years have made us slightly blind to the concern for imperfection which is so obvious in his approach.

A red square on a black background. That picture at the end of *Bad Guy* is first of all an image of an absolute contrast, the meeting of two colours which clash brutally. The red, even though it only represents a small portion of the surface, is more visible than the black. However red and black are as complementary as they are opposite, as autumn to spring. The red is more vivid on the black background, the black is made darker because of the red touch. One can also see in that image a message of hope: in the middle of the night shines a light, a beacon which shows us a land, the warm presence of a home.

It is quite possible that, like the image of the red square on a black background, some films only exist for one fulgurating scene. The whole film would be destined to emphasize the beauty or the violence of one brief moment. Contrast allows the creation of a striking effect. Violence in Kim Ki-duk's films only exist to let out a moment of gentleness… and vice-versa. The propensity for a character to appear nasty has as equivalence only the need to be comforted. The Bad Guy incarnates that contrast. For more than an hour the film explores his brutish external appearance, his wild ways. He remains silent and chilling, like a marble statue lined with scars around his neck. Then, suddenly, he articulates a few words

[5] Hsiung Ping-ming, *Zhang Xu et la calligraphie cursive folle*, Institut de Hautes Etudes Chinoises. Coll. Mémoire de l'IHEC. p161.

in a high-pitched voice, an incredibly painful sound like chalk scratching across a blackboard, or the squeal of a wounded dog dragging its blooded paw. One imagines his vocal cords have been the victim of a blade. His violence and that of the world he hangs around have rendered him mute, like so many of Kim Ki-duk's characters who find in silence the calm that life has denied them.

In Kim Ki-duk's cinema, the essential springs from the violent meeting of two extremes, from characters or feelings diametrically opposed. The contrast explodes then like a hard pebble meeting a fragile window. That language has the effectiveness of the "onomatopoeia founders" of modern Korean literature, to use Patrick Maurus's expression.[6] For example, *From the sea to the adolescents*, a long and essential poem from Ch'oe Namson published in 1908, is not constructed differently. It opens with a series of brutal onomatopoeias evoking the crash of waves.

T'yo...Issok, t'yo... Issok, t'yok, sswa... a
I strike, destroy, I break
mountains high like ***Taesan*** *and rocks like houses*
what is that, what is it
howling, my great strength, you know it, or not
I strike, I break, I destroy.

The sea, unleashed, sweeps over everything, then, in the last verses, the furious ocean lulls the adolescents tenderly.

that ***World*** *those men are all hateful,*
in the ***Middle*** *of that there is only one thing I like*
it's that ***Brave*** *and* ***Pure Adolescents***
throw themselves into my arms as if for a ***Jolly Cuddle***
come ***Adolescents*** *I will embrace you*[7]

Beyond the political message (youth, metaphor for modern Korea), the poem's construction is of a rare brutality. The Chinese characters (here transcribed in bold and capitals) splash onto the reader while the irregular verses break the rhythm. But in a few stanzas, Ch'oe Namson turns the violence against itself, and the crash of waves becomes a gentle rolling. Korean poetry, like its cinema, has been playing a lot with that type of contrast.

Lighting the blue lamp
I strum on my green lute
And mix my pain with the song
Of the caress of the lotus flute.[8]

[6] Patrick Maurus, *La Mutation de la poésie coréenne moderne ou les Onomatopées fondatrices*, Ed. L'Harmattan, 1999.
[7] Trad. Patrick Maurus, Revue *Neige d'Aout* N°5 Automne 2001, p108.
[8] Trad. Patrick Maurus, *Histoire de la littérature Coréenne*. Ed. Ellipses. p43.

15 ▶

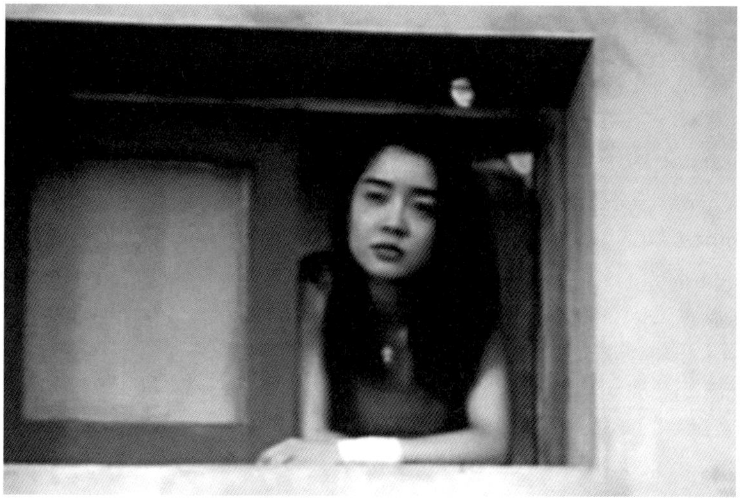

16 ▶

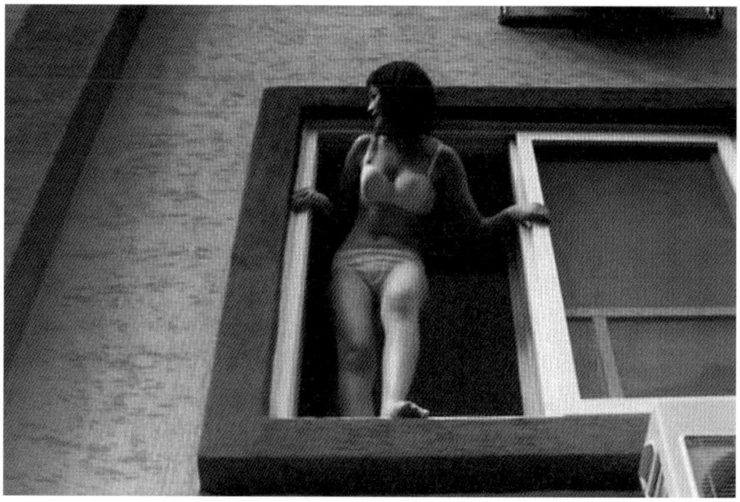

Kim Ki-duk's cinema doesn't function differently than the meeting of the painful song and the gentleness of the flute evoked by the famous poet Hansor Hon in her *sorrow in the boudoir* (17th century). In *The Bow*, one draws from that same lute a sweet chant or a deadly arrow. In the first ending to *Samaritan Girl*, the father murders his daughter, then buries her under the pebbles. For the last time he places the headphones on her which play Erik Satie's *Gymnopédie* and silently contemplates that soothing landscape, bathed in its grey pleasantness.

The director is not so much fascinated by violence as by our desperate efforts to escape it. The characters move forward like the fish in *The Isle* which swims, with half its flesh amputated, or that of *Spring, Summer, Fall, Winter... and Spring* which twists and turns, weighted with its stone. Thugs, prostitutes, thieves, tramps, psychopaths, raped, beaten, wounded, reduced to silence... they are constantly thrown on the ground, dragged in the dirt or towards the deep end. In *Spring, Summer, Fall, Winter... and Spring*, the young monk falls into the river when he's trying to catch the girl bathing, the veiled mother is swallowed by a hole in the ice, like the boat which lets in water. All are trying to escape that fatal movement, and to rise above: to pass to the other side, to open the *Big Blue Door* (*paran daemun*, the original title of *Birdcage Inn*) and find an *Empty House* (*pin jip*, original title of *3-iron*) or a soothing landscape, an *Isle*.

One morning in 1969, Kim Ki-duk left his village and family house. He was leaving for Seoul, like so many Koreans at the time. He was heading towards a harsh life, that of factories, then army and street. That brutal uprooting of a part of the population has been one of the main sources of modern Korean aesthetics. Films and novels will tell the story of many dreams shattered on the edges of Seoul. In traditional melodrama, urban poverty generated noble feelings of courage. Kim Ki-duk announces in this very first shot of his first film that misery doesn't generate compassion but indifference, if not cruelty. A man throws himself in the Han river, in the cold urban night. A tramp takes off his clothes and jumps. He comes out, a wallet in his hand, letting the man drown. Seoul has invented anonymity. The village was a space where everyone knew everyone. In Seoul, the body has nothing but trading value, is nothing more than a prey for crocodiles. The city gathers together anonymous bodies and generates emotionless desires for flesh.

"Do you know what is the most marvellous and desirable thing in the eyes of the young country folk who've gone to Seoul for the first time? What they desire, whatever anyone says, are not the lights which are lit in the evening at the windows of the buildings, but the people who come and go in those lights and what is new is the fact that a pretty girl is

17 ▼

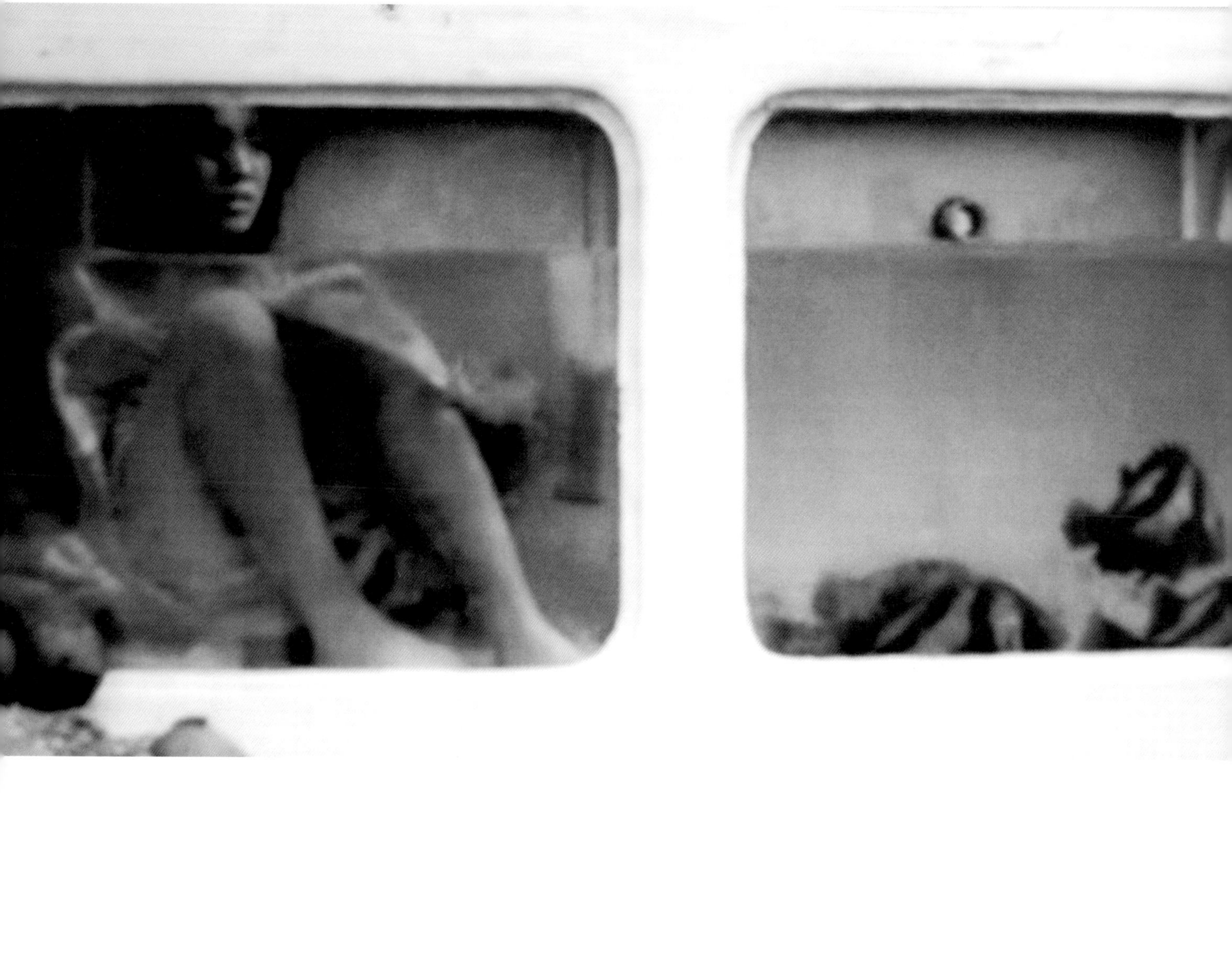

standing one centimetre away from you in the bus. To be able to touch for a moment the skin of the girls' wrists, or even rub against their thighs..." Kim Sûng'ok wrote in the short story *Winter 64*.[9] Everything is summed up in one word: the city is the space for prostitution.

> ...
> *I'm leaving*
> *Don't cry*
> *I'm leaving*
> *Behind the white hills, the black and dry hills*
> *Following the long dusty road which leads to Seoul*
> *I'm going to sell my body...*[10]

From that point of view, the cinema of Kim Ki-duk will only have pushed a bit further the feelings and themes already existing, often proving to be a moralist. *Samaritan Girl* or *Bad Guy* are the portraits of those cities where anonymity makes prostitution so easy. They especially evoke the nostalgia for the "native land" (the omnipresent notion of *Ko hyang* in Korea), that place one is searching for but which often no longer exists. The torn photo in *Bad Guy* represents that lost native land, that time of innocence forever erased. In *Samaritan Girl*, the policemen takes his prostituted daughter to the *ko hyang* on her mother's grave. He puts her back in a pure space, facing mountains and rivers, and nature's majesty. Pushing the bogged-down car, she rediscovers the value of effort, like a therapy. In the same way, the murderer in *Spring, Summer, Fall, Winter... and Spring* comes back to the temple and washes away his urban life by living according to the cycle of nature. Kim Ki-Duk's heroes only suffer from that, that definitive split with a past forever gone, from an impossibility to go back to their origins.[11] Loose and unattached, they are lost letters in *Address Unknown*. Bewildered, they find shelter *on the other side*, in nests, enclosed, silent and warm spaces. The pleasure of voyeurism in Kim Ki-duk, in the peep-show of *Wild Animals* or *Bad Guy* is not so much linked to the fact of seeing an exciting body through the glass, than to imprisonment. The voyeur doesn't *come* from seeing but from not being seen, being out of reach, sheltered from the world, behind a two-way mirror. Kim Ki-duk's voyeur is a refugee, the peep-show booth is no different from the fish tank in which the victim of *Coast Guard* bleeds to death, from the little floating houses of *The Isle*, from the monastery drifting on the lake in *Spring, Summer, Fall, Winter... and Spring* or the boat in *The Bow*. Still playing with contrasts, one faces again the feeling of well-being linked to the lost landscape, the immensity of the mountains of the abandoned *ko hyang,* by locking oneself in the smallest possible space. One finds in cramped spaces the immensity of the

[9] Patrick Maurus, *Passeport pour Séoul*. Ed. Actes Sud, 2002.

[10] Kim Chi-ha *The Road to Seoul*. English translation by David R. McCann in *The Middle Hour: Selected Poems of Kim Chi Ha*, Stradfordville, NY: Human Rights Publishing Group, 1980, p19.

[11] A trait common to a great number of contemporary Korean director. The symbolic image being that of the hero (Lee Chang-dong) in *Peppermint Candy*, who shouts at the train which hurtles towards him: "I'm going backwards!"

sky, not in the sense of a Christian paradise but in the Korean sense which supports the idea of "native land": *"My characters turn to the sky in moments of crisis for the sky is witness and judge of our History, the place of our ancestors and gods. It is thus an original source comparable to the native land*[12]", says Yun Hûngkil, author of the novel, *The Monsoon*.

The two last shots of *The Isle* can be seen as the image-matrix of Kim Ki-duk's cinema. A criminal hunted down by the police moves, half-naked, in a gigantic swamp. In the end he finds shelter in a grove of reeds. The camera suddenly takes on a vertiginous aerial point of view. The naked woman is lying down in a boat full of water. On her pubis, a tuft of grass is floating. It is obviously the reeds in which the hunted man has disappeared. The island which gives its title to the film is the woman's sex. Man only aspires to land on it, to pass to the other side to escape brutality.

Even if one has to pay her, the woman is a shelter (one sees it very clearly in the attitude of some of the "clients" in *Samaritan Girl*). All scales are turned upside down. The lake becomes a boat, the thicket of reeds a tuft of grass or an island. The image of the boat full of water reappears in *Samaritan Girl* and *Spring, Summer, Fall, Winter... and Spring*. It shows us that there is neither big nor small, neither container nor contained. The boat holds the lake, the small absorbs the big like *"the reflection of the distant mountains in the dragonfly's pupil"*[13].

The most violent, furious heroes aspire to land on a mysterious island, a secret shelter which would have the shape of a red square in an ocean of black. "The enjoyment of being enclosed reaches its paroxysm when, from the bosom of this unbroken inwardness, it is possible to watch, through a large window-pane, the outside vagueness of the waters, and thus define, in a single act, the inside by means of its opposite."[14], wrote Roland Barthes about Captain Nemo. The Nautilus in *Crocodile* would be, for example, that tiny bourgeois living-room (sofa, painting on the wall...) that the thug has prepared at the bottom of the river, and where he will go and chain himself to his beloved at the end of the film. In the same vein the old tramp dies, locked in a coffee machine... In his first films Kim Ki-duk seems embarrassed by that paradox: one can escape violence by locking oneself up but one suffocates, one drowns in one's fish tank. He will find an answer in the spiritual world. For the monk of *Spring, Summer, Fall, Winter... and Spring,* as for the burglar of *3-iron*, it's not a question of locking oneself up physically but looking for isolation in oneself through meditation and physical exercises, a mix of dance, martial arts and tai-chi: *"The apprehension of heaven by man doesn't happen elsewhere than in the man himself. Heaven is not beyond the man, an elsewhere only reachable through a big leap (death or*

[12] Interviewed by Cathy Rapin and Im Hye-Gyong in "Treize écrivains coréens" Centre National du livre, 1995, p77.
[13] Celebrated Haiku.
[14] Roland Barthes, *Mythologies*, Points Seuil, 1957, p82. (English translation by Annette Lavers, Paladin, 1973, p66.)

grace): Heaven is the most authentic part of the man as a being capable of transcending himself more and more in his own humanity."[15]

The end of *Spring, Summer, Fall, Winter... and Spring* repeats that of *The Isle* by giving it a Buddhist interpretation. The monk, harnessed to a heavy stone, painfully climbs the mountain, holding a statue of Bodhisattva. Having reached the summit one suddenly realizes that the lake one thought was immense, is only a little pond in the middle of an infinite landscape, not much bigger than the hole the monk was boring in the ice with an axe. The man who climbs the mountain with his statue makes the same effort as the fish attached to its stone. The Buddhist concept of "*tong*" reappears here, that one can rather unpoetically translate by the word "interpenetration". Interpenetration of the seasons, the characters (the disciple becomes the master), the men and the animals, and above all, the big and the small. That great circulation between the elements of the landscape is represented by the lake. Water obeys the cycle of seasons, it turns into ice before opening up to transparency by becoming liquid again...: *"The whole spectacle of nature – and first of all that of the sky – makes us more sensitive to what manifests itself as a* contrast[16]*: the spontaneous limpidity, transparent and infinite, or the obscurity born from the screen (as soon as the mist appears). The alternation to the work makes all reality vibrate on that double mode: subtilization/reification, fluidity/density, transparency (of the landscape)/opacity (of the obstacle)*[17]". To pass to the other side, to pass through the double swing-door which opens onto the lake, allows the adoption of that natural rhythm, the contrasts of the great alternation *yin – yang*. It is the only way to experience again the feeling of plenitude and the lost *Ko hyang*. The monk manages to leap across the frozen lake on which the woman was sinking, the old sailor in *The Bow* loses himself in the sea and the sky. The character in *3-iron* escapes the heavy burden of the world. He becomes invisible, floats like a spirit, creates in himself the emptiness of deserted houses. He says to us that all of Kim Ki-duk heroes, who were desperately looking for a shelter, were blinded by their own pain. In the end the shelter was in them, like the red square is contained in the black.

Epilogue: The other side of the doors

In 1974, Nam June Paik put the final touch to one of his most famous installations, *TV Buddha*: a big statue of Buddha was seated facing a camera linked to a TV monitor. The effect was striking: Buddha was looking at himself on television! Has God become a cathodic narcissist? In reality, Paik wanted to say that Buddha doesn't succeed in escaping his own corporeity to rise above his materiality[18]. But the work will slowly evolve, and exist

[15] Anne Cheng, *Histoire de la pensée chinoise*, Seuil, 1997, p173.
[16] My underlining.
[17] François Jullien, *Procès ou Création. Une introduction à la pensée chinoise.* Ed. du Seuil, 1989, p28.
[18] See: Edith Decker-Phillips *Paik Video.* Ed. Barrytown, New-York, pp74-79.

in various versions, following Buddha's meditation through the years. In 1982, Nam June Paik installed *TV Buddha No.X* in the Whitney Museum of American Art in New York. The screen was placed this time on a pile of earth which represented a mountain. *TV Buddha No.X* tells how Buddha, after seven years of meditations, has finally passed to the other side. He has "entered the mountain" (in Korean, *ip-san*, "to enter the mountain", means to become a monk). The Buddha lets himself be absorbed totally by the elements. He dominates the mountain but at the same time, he is dominated by it. He is at the same time inside and outside the landscape. Paik has turned a video *circuit* into an illustration of a cycle (circuit) of seasons and elements which interpenetrate. *TV Buddha* tells a familiar journey, a journey described in that famous text sometimes attributed to the Chinese monk, Ching Yuan: "*Before having studied for thirty years, I used to see the mountain as mountain and the water as water. When I managed a slightly deeper knowledge, I reached the point when I saw that the mountain was not the mountain and the water was not the water. When I managed an even deeper knowledge, I saw that the mountain is water and the water is mountain. But now, having the true knowledge, I am at peace. For I see again the mountain as mountain and the water as water*[19]". Nam June Paik's camera also allowed the visitor to see the Buddha inside the mountain, meaning to see the mountain as it really is, in its globality, at the same time container and contained.

Kim Ki-duk is trying to make of cinema a similar spiritual quest. The matter is to get rid of false images, of all illusions, to change the viewpoint, to pass through the door and reach a kind of just and clear vision. For cinema alone allows the biggest to enter the smallest, to turn upside down all scales. Those scales turned upside down, those bodies in turn huge and tiny, which had upset the first spectators at the beginning of the Twentieth Century are in no way an artificial special effect, or a new language to decipher. They are the vision of the world at its rightest, the only vision which doesn't lock the elements in fixed proportions. In the camera as in Buddha's eyes, there is neither big nor small. Cinema doesn't distort the world. It gives it back its exact proportions. In film after film, Kim Ki-duk learns, from the other side of the camera, to see the mountain as mountain and the water as water.

[19] Translated from the Chinese by Ynhui Park in *Essais Philosophiques et Littéraires*, Seoul National University Press, 1997, p53-54.

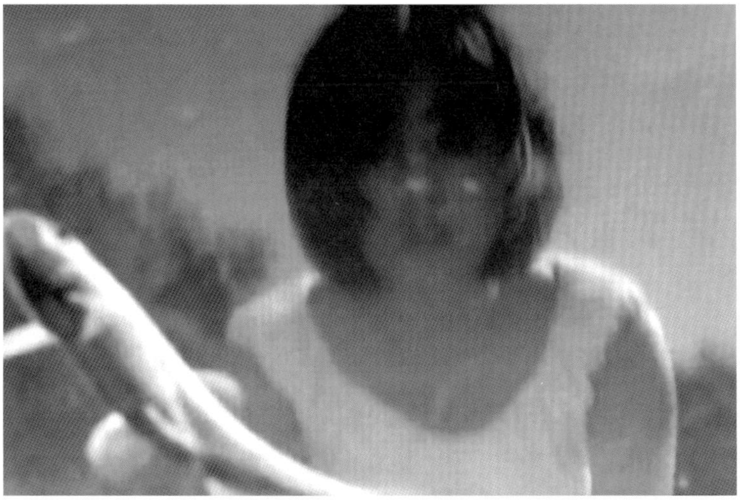

◀ 18

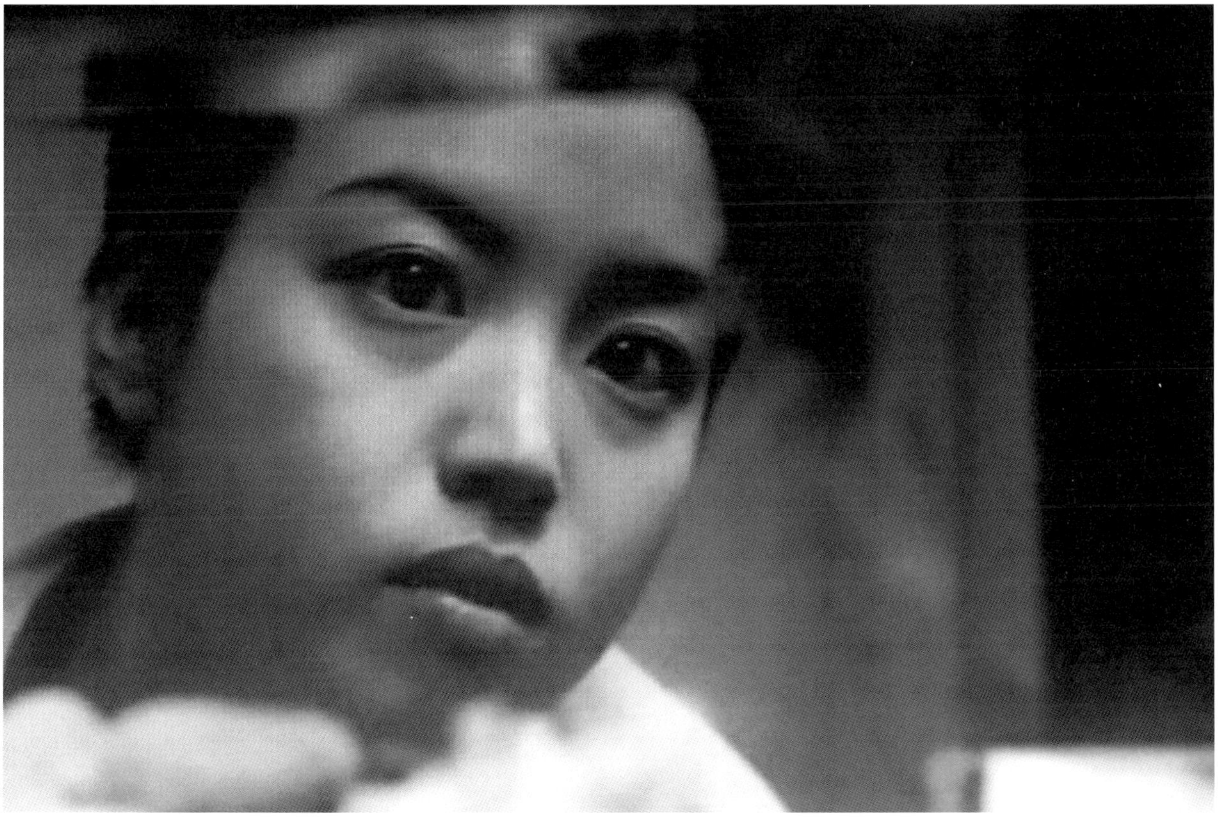

◀ 19

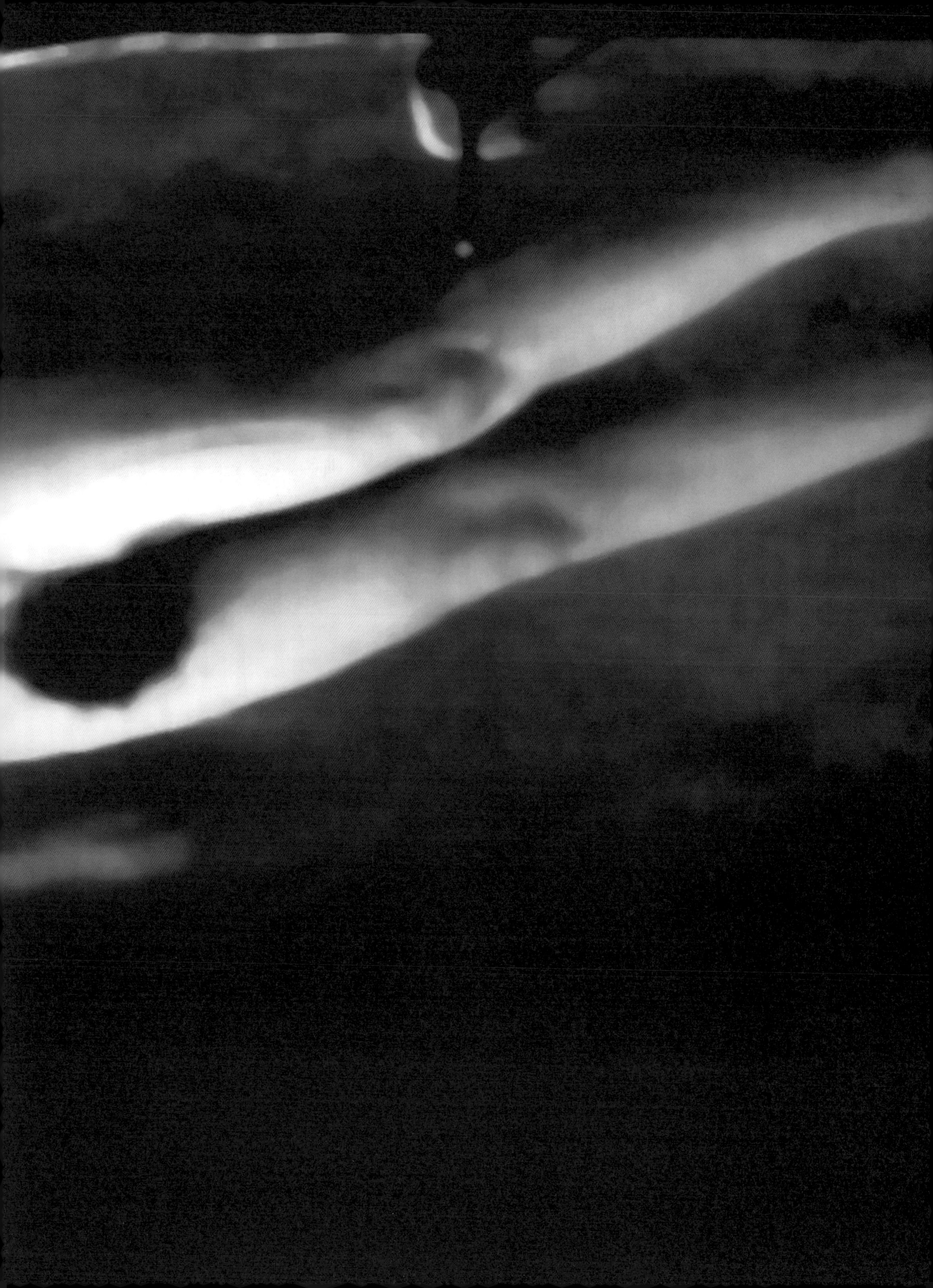

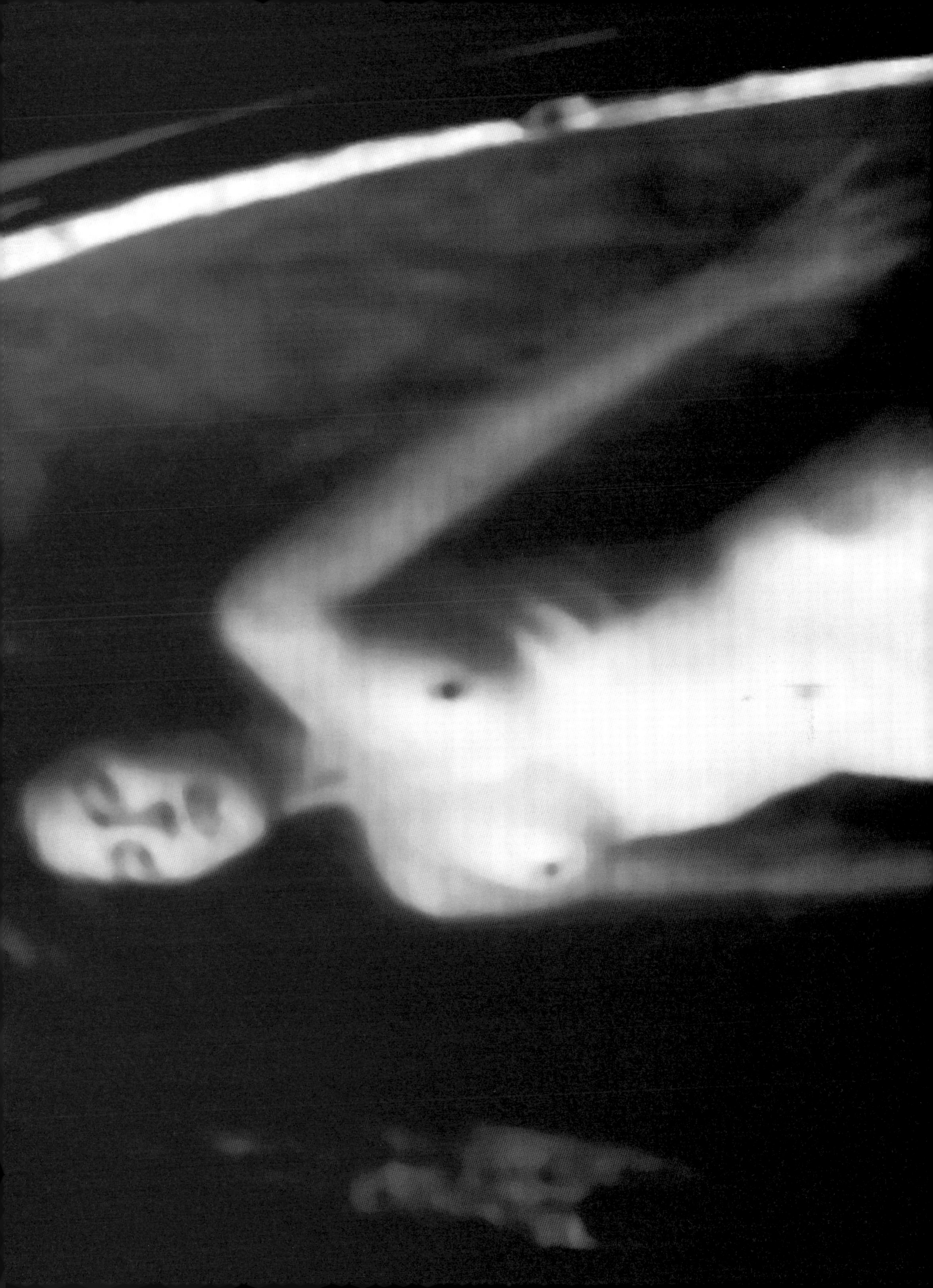

20 ▲

21 ▶

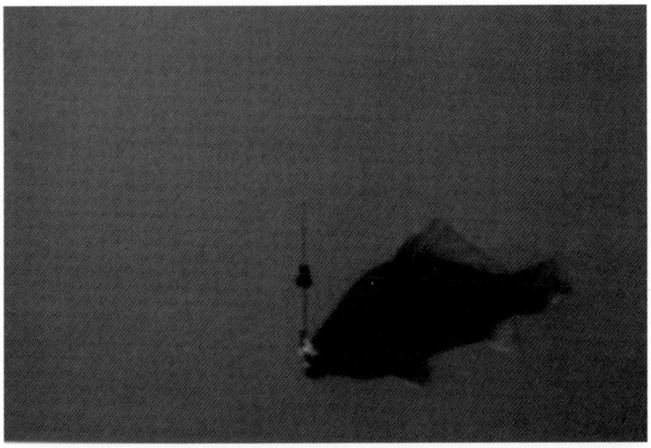

22 ▶

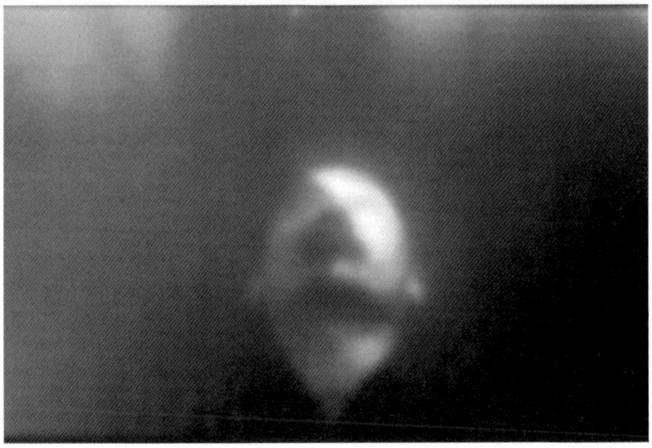

23 ▶

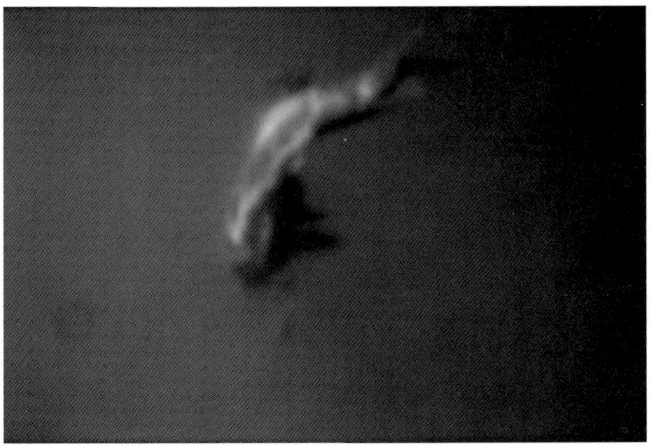

KIM KI-DUK, SERIAL PAINTER

Flayed, traumatised and turning red... In Kim Ki-duk's films, bodies are presented in idyllic and lush landscapes worthy of romantic postcards sent from Korea. But the best dramas are played between the flourishing mountains crests and the blue surfaces of the lakes and oceans.

Beneath Kim Ki-duk's scalpel, bodies, and the people who live in them, are taken from life with a surgical preoccupation for detail, an art of precision and a staging of suffering which is all Far-Eastern refinement.

Through a filmography as injected with blood as on the edge, Kim Ki-duk shows the still-oozing wounds of a Korean society maltreated by its history. Insular and divided, in search of harmony, it seeks more than ever to affirm its vivaciousness and to abandon its shackles. But, in order to free oneself, one has to first feel alive.

Surgeon, anthropologist or sociologist... Kim Ki-duk is a bit of each. Who else could have probed better than him the depths of the Korean soul? His personal journey, as chaotic as original, has left him constantly oscillating between the physical and mystical world, a tense journey which partly explains his films. From the forgotten village where he was born, in the Kyonsang province, in the heart of the mountains, to Seoul, the capital of South Korea, where he arrived with his parents aged nine, it's the dichotomy between the countryside and town that is created in his mind. The agricultural school he was forced to attend, though he would have liked to continue studying at senior school, then factory work at seventeen, and finally a five-year military service stint with the Marines, in a world as testing on the body as on the nervous system... are experiences which forced him to live through a large array of physical sensations. Then it was time to devote himself to the spiritual world, as a redemption, giving himself to contemplation. He withdrew to a monastery as he became interested in painting.

In 1990, he left to study art in France and become himself. A fine observer of the human soul, he sharpened his brushes, knives and pencils and made his way as a street artist. Working with models, Kim Ki-duk sketched characters who, though trying hard to remain frozen and be seen as beautiful images, had no intention of being sensible. From extreme serenity to extreme pain, Kim Ki-duk takes us now on a tour around an ever-surprising gallery of living portraits in which the plant world, through its wildest landscapes, as well as the animal kingdom in all its splendour, participate. With works one imagines painted with human fluids and blood, Kim Ki-duk undertakes a vivisection of the social flesh.

Elements of a pictorial crime: incarnate paintings

The three colours of the key chart (red, green, blue) appear in the opening minutes of *The Bow* (2005), Kim Ki-duk's twelfth film, as if to indicate that we have crossed to the other side, into a fictionalized zone situated between the pictorial world and the film world. It is an anonymous male hand that appends as a kind of seal those three dots of colour, with a paintbrush, on the temple of a young child who is taken in by an old man living on a barge.

Immediately, the eye of the serial-painter has tattooed the skin of one of his preys. For, in the audio-visual world, Kim Ki-duk is self-taught. He is essentially a painter who draws from models, and who has replaced his easel, pencils and paint brushes with a movie camera, and, like any self-respecting serial painter, Kim Ki-duk has ironically represented himself through that pencil dipped in blood that the street artist in *Real Fiction* sharpens carefully before executing his victims. Once the crimes are committed, the same pencil is used to execute portraits in graphite with fluidity and precision. As a back drop, as in all his films, Korean society with its limits, its troubles and traumas appears, then, by extension, the whole of humanity. In a few large strokes, or in subtle silky little touches, with lightness, naiviety and gentleness, or with the bite of a furious pencil stroke, Kim Ki-duk depicts a cruel and violent world where bodies are sold for very little money, and current business settled in blood.

His weapons, often improvised, offer diversity: fishhooks (*The Isle*), a simple sheet of paper rolled into a point to attack a vital spot, a bevelled piece of glass (*Bad Guy*)... everything that slices, cuts or pierces the flesh is good enough to use.

And, as with painting, one is never short of colours for Kim Ki-duk has a predilection for red which he takes directly from its source: the heart of blood vessels. And one can read the future in the blood as others do with coffee grounds or DNA. The character's intentions, like their rage, their resentments, their pains and problems of communication measure up to the blood spilt.

That one fights over a stolen painting, that one paints or has a nose bleed, there is always something to redden the work in the painter's studio that one of the characters in *Wild Animals*, the South Korean artist-crook, visits in Paris. And in the public park, it doesn't matter if the sculpture is Camille Claudel's, a few trails of blood are enough to take it away from its corpse-like whiteness and revive it.

Blood is a pictorial substance which represents the characters and imprints their vital energy right to the extreme, whether it be in the suffering of dogs beaten to death for gastronomic purposes in *Address Unknown* and whose blood pigments the mud, or that of an unbearable abortion in *Coast Guard*, or else that of proof of pleasure and the deflowered hymen for the girl in *The Bow*, who bleeds between her legs in her virginal child bride's dress… After all, only the living can bleed.

And those devious, wounded, tormented characters who pause at length between pain and pleasure are the models of a studio of morpho-psycho-sociology that Kim Ki-duk would direct. Analysed from every angle, sounded, closely examined, their organs on edge, they walk in the foreground.

Through Kim Ki-duk's films, we visit the tableaux of a Korean malaise whose truth the director has chosen to exacerbate. And he starts with his own truth, by cultivating the art of self portrait, if not of autobiography. With *Coast Guard* it is his experience in the marines which is reviewed and fantasized about. His filmography helps us to find him at various periods of his life. In order to identify him, we sometimes have to look for the serial-painter who has wriggled his way into the narrative. Thus, in *Address Unknown*, one of the teenagers, Jihum, is the son of a South Korean war veteran. He is in love with a one-eyed girl who doesn't accept her handicap. When he hands her a realistic portrait he has made of her, she tears it violently. This adolescent boy is, in reality, Kim Ki-duk. In *Wild Animals*, the director depicts his own experience as a penniless painter in Europe and shows how one can easily be dragged into the spiral of the mafia in order to pay the rent for one's studio. In *Real Fiction*, the artist drawing the model transcends himself and takes revenge, as we have already seen earlier. More contemplative, *Spring, Summer, Fall, Winter… and Spring* refers to that period when he had retreated into the calm of a monastery: he even films himself in his own role at the end of that masterpiece of four seasons and five periods.

The unreasoned catalogue of Twentieth Century art

From reality to extreme reality, even to sur-reality, Kim Ki-duk's filmography lets us glance through the pages of an unreasoned catalogue of Twentieth Century art.

In frameworks with a sometimes Impressionist flavour, human beings anchored in their Realism fight against their own demons with Expressionism, and most often tip over into Fauvism. But through all those sequences which sometimes take on the ways of performances, it's always life which is expressed with the same vigour.

The unreal doors to the floating monastery in *Spring, Summer, Fall, Winter… and Spring* (2003) open each season on a new tableau. An Impressionist canvas which the spectator enters each time with sheer delight. The incredible views of those landscapes, as if straight from Eden, force us to contemplate and feel blissful. It is a variation on the same theme, with a landscape which traverses the seasons of the year and life. One goes through the stages in a boat, rocked by the water's undulations.

While painters like Manet, Monet or Renoir proceeded with small fine touches to celebrate the natural panoramas and played with the variations of light through the day, Kim Ki-duk has chosen to use the seasons for his initiative fable. But each of his films has the same preoccupation to represent nature in its most paradisiac aspects, sometimes almost to the point of being naive. Nature is presented in its best light, appeasing and generous, in the views of the floating houses in *The Isle*, in the autumnal public park in *Samaritan Girl* or that, more spring-like, in *Bad Guy*. Even the military camp located at the border with North Korea in *Coast Guard*, a zone with the reputation of being the most militarized in the world, looks just like a tourist site where nature lovers don't hesitate to have their picture taken. Danger and violence are more likely to be found in the city. But one can also lose one's life in those apparently inoffensive landscapes. Or be its captive. But it's a question then of going back to one's roots. Yeo-Jin, one of the teenage prostitutes in *Samaritan Girl* is taken back by her father to nature without her realising. When, on the shore of the river, her father paints pebbles in yellow to design a circuit for his daughter to learn to drive, in that deserted landscape he offers us an installation piece worthy of Land Art. And though the young girl is not shown floating at the surface of the water but buried in the silt at the river's edge, her face, probably asleep for all eternity, gives her the calm air of the Pre-Raphaelite "Ophelia", by the British painter, John Everett Millais.

After the divine, enchanting and redeeming countryside, comes the city, extreme and infernal. It is a nest of Fauvism and Expressionism in which Kim Ki-duk explicitly summons a few figures dear to him. Let's start with the fleeting evocation of Kees van Dongen in *Wild Animals*: one of the female characters is very attached to a portrait, that of a Parisian woman with a hat, signed by the Fauvist master, known at the end of the Nineteenth Century in Paris for painting the portraits of cabaret female artists and defending the cause of poverty-stricken prostitutes. We cannot be surprised at that wink of the director towards the painter.

But nothing compares to the place occupied by Egon Schiele. That painter is regularly mentioned, to the extent that he becomes a recurrent motif. Kim Ki-duk pays constant tribute to the artist whom undoubtedly he considers on equal footing. For having produced

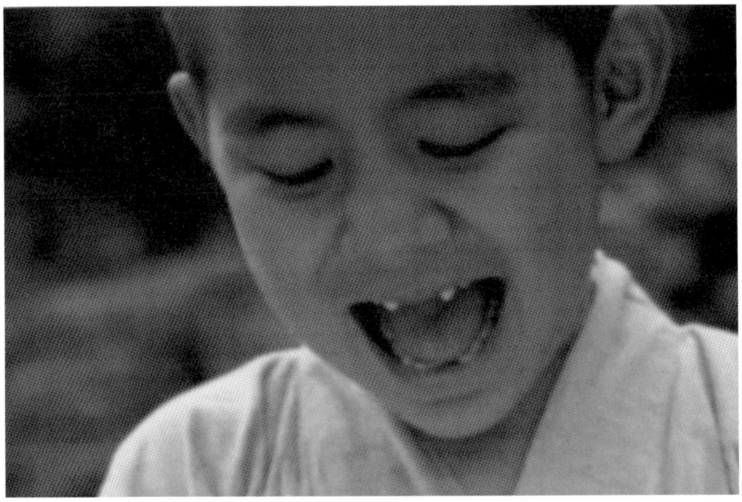
◀ 24

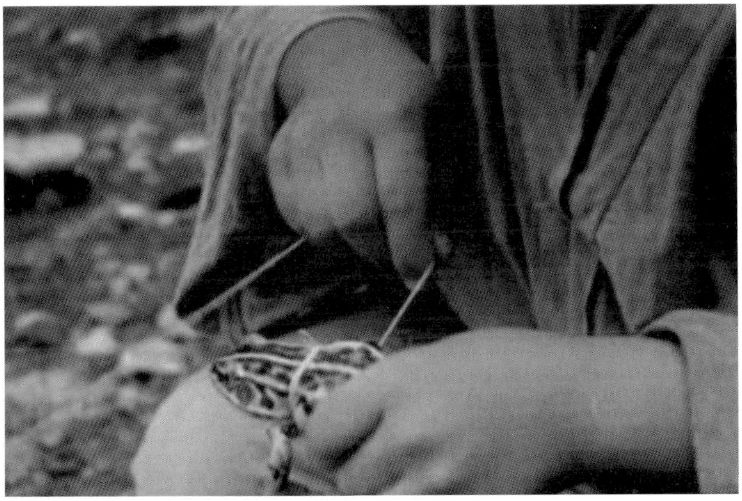
◀ 25

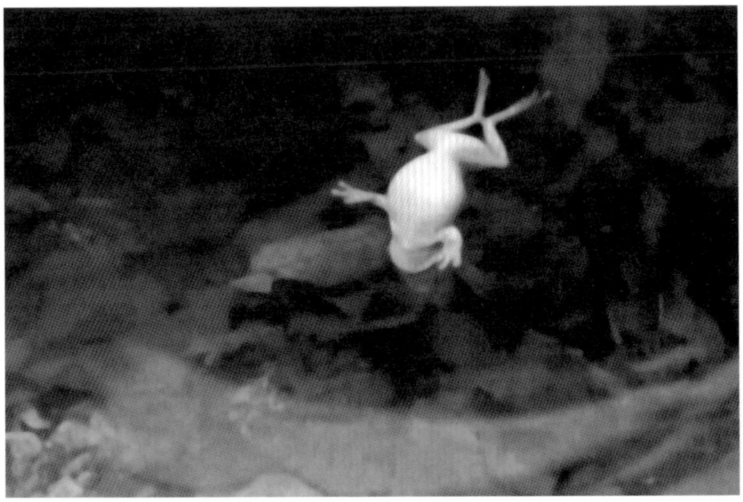
◀ 26

highly erotic drawings, so-called "immoral" for the time, Schiele, that virtuoso of Expressionist representation of the bodies had, among other things, been accused of rape and the seduction of minors, before being imprisoned at the beginning of the Twentieth Century. His work, sensual and raw, predominantly characters on a rough background, as well as his tormented life, make him a romantic figure with which Kim Ki-duk can easily identify. The Viennese painter is even almost at the heart of some intrigues for, in *Bad Guy*, Sun-hwa, the young female student, is drawn into a plot and ends up becoming a prostitute after browsing a monograph on Schiele whose page she has torn out before running away. The drawing represented a couple having sex, as if a premonition of the fate reserved for her. As for Hang-gi, the man who lures with Machiavellism that student on the street, his image is from time to time superimposed with the genuine self-portrait of Schiele. Like the two young sisters who posed together for Schiele and whose portrait is ever-present in *Birdcage Inn*, the two young rival women in that film become closer and closer until they split and appear united by the same blood. When an illegitimate couple makes love on a bed of roses (*Real Fiction*) or elsewhere, we are always reminded of the settings of some of Schiele's paintings. For, after painting, we can still remain at the heart of Viennese sensations… since scenes where pain and haemoglobin feature heavily immediately remind us of the Actionists.

Sometimes the living want to be as hard as stone and attempt inertia. In a public park the teenage girls in *Samaritan Girl* sit next to a series of hyper-realistic statues whose uniform whiteness connects us to the art of statuary and evokes, in passing, a certain family ideal. The very colourful young girls slide in next to them and emphasize their very own existence, their lack of family references and the fact that they are themselves made of flesh and blood, though undoubtedly in full disincarnation. A bit like that enigmatic Korean girl without a name in *Wild Animals* who endlessly undulates in the peep show booth. Though alive, she looks more like an automaton. At the opposite is Corinne, in the same film, who is trying to erase all trace of her life by sliding in as a *trompe l'oeil* in the landscape. That young Hungarian woman, half-naked, whose body is dipped in whiting, plays at being the Venus de Milo. She competes with the real statues in a public park, among which is one by Camille Claudel that she dreams of possessing. A living sculpture mounted on a makeshift pedestal, Corinne is also the sexual slave of a man who doesn't hesitate to beat her with a frozen mackerel. She ends by finishing off her tormentor with the fatal blow of a mackerel in his groin. This beautiful metaphor derived from *maquereau* (meaning pimp and mackerel in French) is a well-deserved ending for that man who has constantly behaved like a pimp with his fiancee, and about whom Kim Ki-duk makes us genuinely laugh. For Kim Ki-duk can be humorous as well as capable of the greatest poetry. *Spring, Summer, Fall, Winter... and Spring* presents us with a magnificent sequence which is between Surrealism and a feline version of Body Art: the monk grabs the white cat, dips the tip of its tail in black ink and, using it as a brush, casually writes on the floor a text composed of ideogrammes that his ex-disciple will have to carve out with a knife.

Body Art and Living Art, we are not surprised to learn that Kim Ki-duk's method of shooting also owes more to performance than to contemplation, since the films are shot in minimal time and at a sustained rhythm. Just the necessary time, the one of life.

Tests and prints: photographic revelations

Between pictorial representation and life there is also photography, a medium with much presence in Kim Ki-duk's cinema, an art which the director accords special care, without us ever knowing for sure how highly he thinks of it.

After all, we witness the murder of the photographer in *Real Fiction*. The author of that symbolic death is of course the street artist. Through that metaphor, the two art forms, that naturally fight over the representation of reality, have in a way provoked each other in a duel beneath our eyes. It's an old quarrel that dates back to the end of the Nineteenth Century and the invention of photography: an episode on which the director returns here with caustic humour.

Apart from that, each time photographs appear, they offer the spectacle of an uncertain identity, damaged, muddy, scattered. An integrity to recompose, if possible. In *Address Unknown*, it is the historic memory which is stained with mud, like the two Koreas, those two sisters at war. Indeed one finds a family photo in a South Korean village, at a place where North Koreans have taken shelter.

As for Sun-hwa, the young student led astray in *Bad Guy*, she has found a torn photo on the beach. Though she tries her best to reconstruct the picture, the couple represented have no face, no identity.... just like the couple she makes with Hang-gi, her pimp. With the photo placed on her mirror, Sun-hwa gradually finds the colours. The features of the face appear as the couple reveal themselves and each of the protagonists lets their feelings for the other show. The mute woman in *3-iron*, abused and reduced to a kind of conjugal slavery by her wealthy husband, finds a grain of love and humanity with Tae-suk, that enigmatic character who enters the flats temporarily deserted by their occupants. She follows him in his trips until the duo arrive at a photographer who has taken the picture of

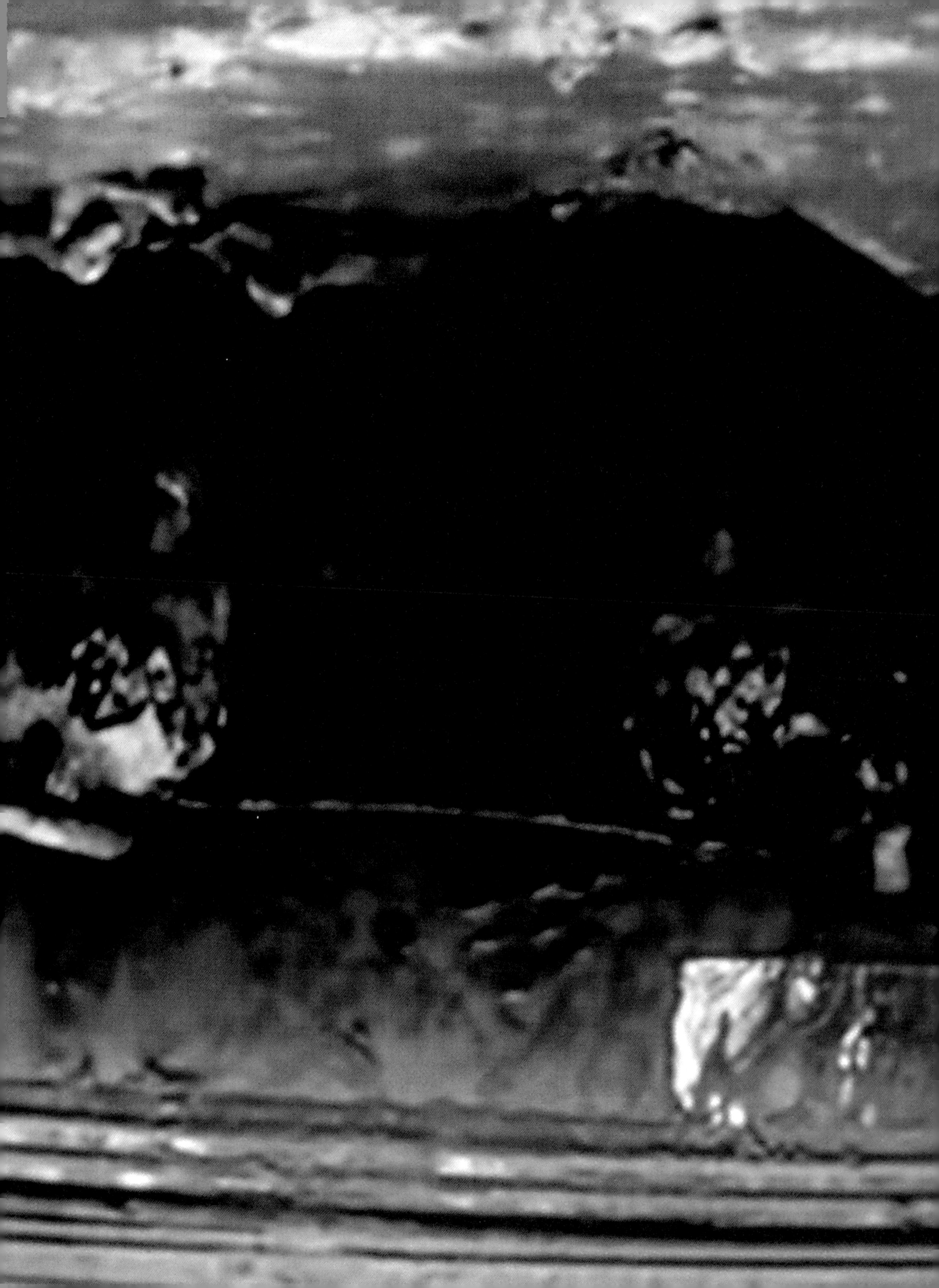

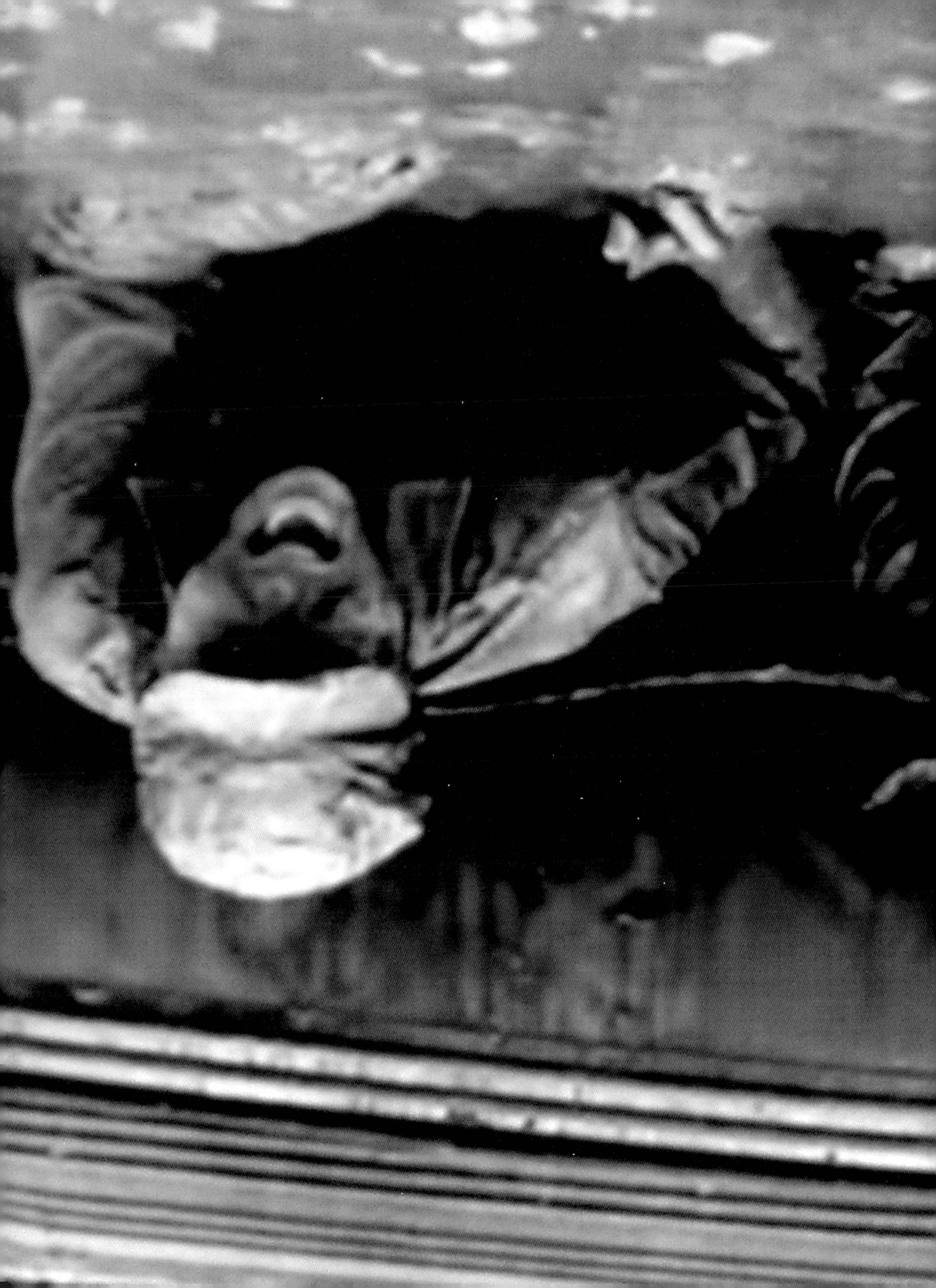

27 ▲

that girl. With a pair of scissors, she hastens to do a jigsaw puzzle of that overly neat picture of herself. She makes a sort of Cubist work which she replaces in its frame. In that same film, the ritual of the intruder, Tae-suk, consists in taking a photo of himself in front of a portrait of the flat's occupants, as if to enter a family history from which he is excluded, or to simply prove his existence. For it's only ghosts which do not register on film, and despite appearances, Tae-suk is not a ghost. Through that photographic act, which is also a refined exercise in Conceptual Art, operates a beautiful photo within a photo within... Everywhere else, each time the characters try to get together, or separate, if it's not through a camera, it is mirrors and other reflecting surfaces such as water, which undertake to reveal the reality of a relationship. The characters spend time taking pictures of each other in Kim Ki-duk's universe. They step as much as they can behind the lens, like the two friends in *Samaritan Girl* who capture their image on their mobile phone, or reflected as a couple on the surface of the water, or on a computer screen. As for the young girl in *The Bow* who takes photographs of the one for whom her heart beats, that gesture is as much a mute love declaration as a extra means to seduce him.

Photography is above all a new pretext to frame, centre, control and discipline emotions and feelings. Bodies appear through fences, cages and barbed wire. The soldiers parked in their camp in *Coast Guard* appear behind their fences in a world one feels is like a concentration camp. And who better than the smiling girl who jumps through the window frame in *Samaritan Girl* to show us her suffocation, her need to leave the frame. The doors to the monastery in *Spring, Summer, Fall, Winter... and Spring* open and close on various animated tableaux. The chapters of a life. Furthermore, the monk, when he wants to end his life, cuts out little bits of paper on which he writes the word "closed" and sticks it on his mouth, his eyes and nostrils. He obstructs those orifices, ceases to feel, smell, and finally to breath.

Prison-body and attempts at escaping

In Kim Ki-duk's films, the body is a prison one seeks to escape. That is explained by a historic reality: in Korea there is the strong presence of the American army. But one is also the prisoner of one's nature, one's desires and, above all, one's needs, especially sexual.

The body especially is the place for all suffering and if one grapples with all extremities possible it is to better to escape it or prove that one is really and truly made of flesh and blood. Sado-masochism is present in all its cuts, all its burns, and sutures. In *The Isle*, the

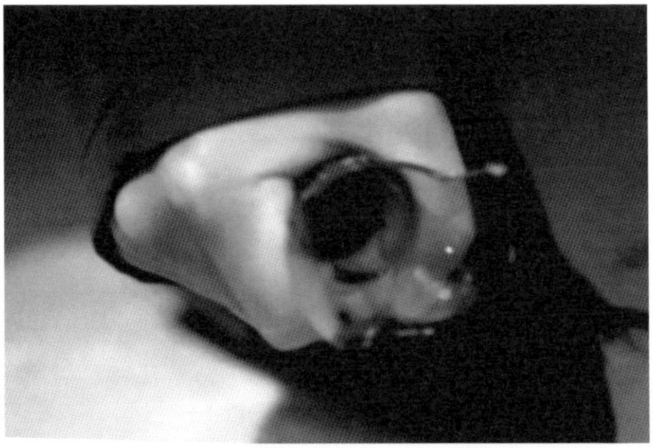
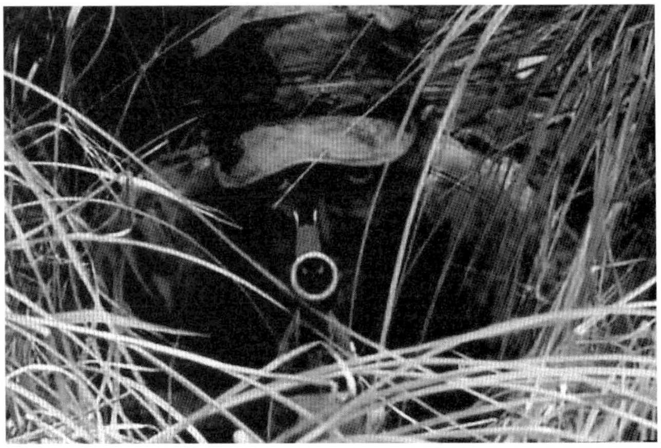
◀28 ◀29

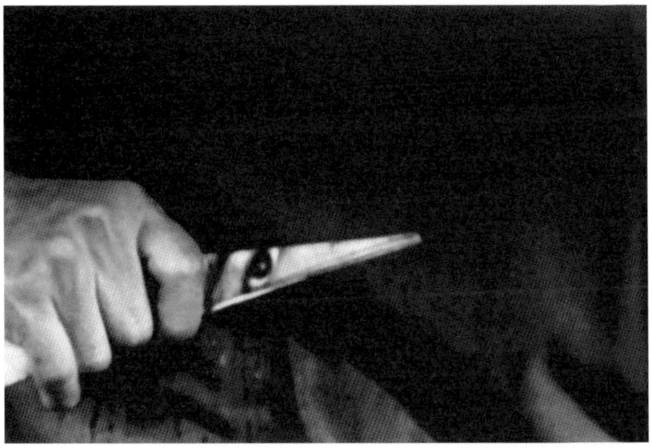
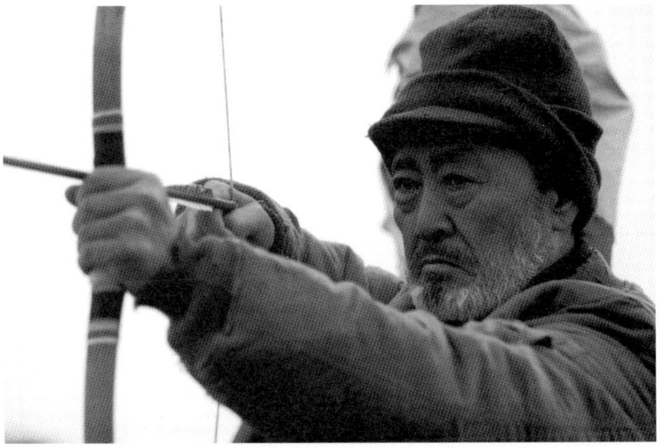
◀30 ◀31

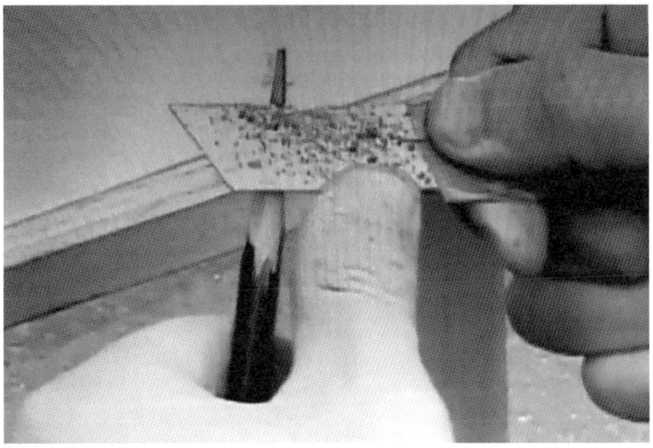
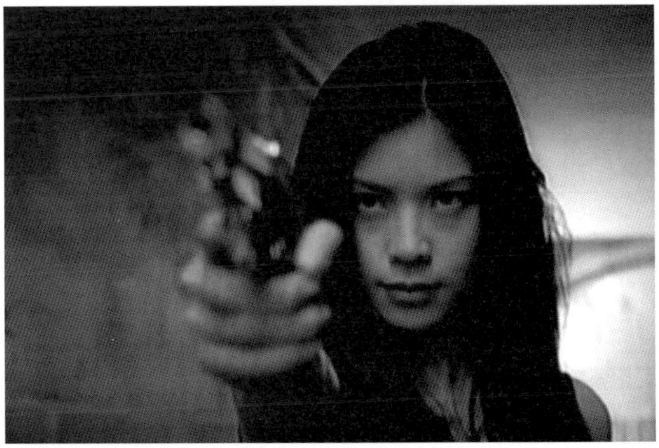
◀32 ◀33

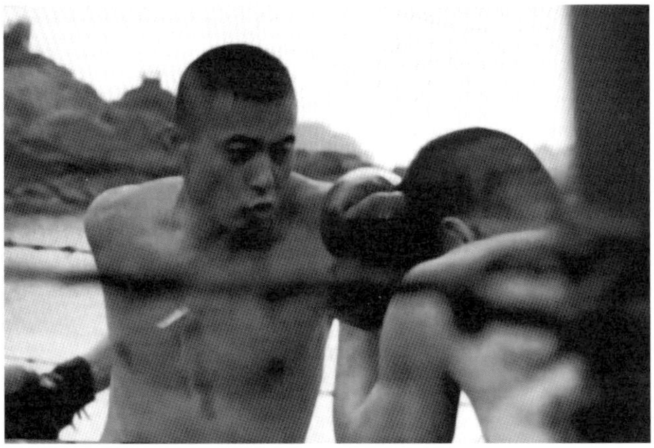
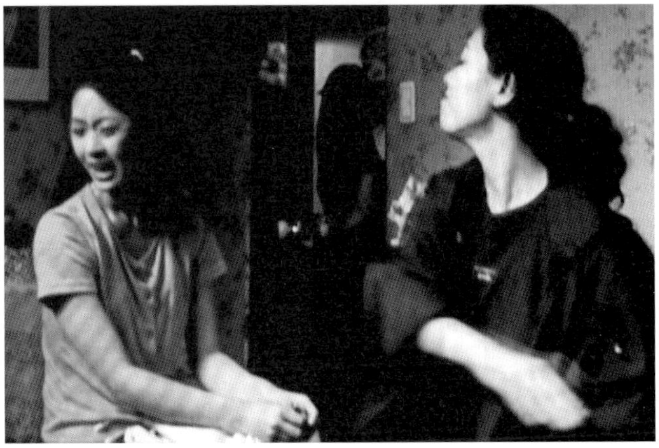
◀34 ◀35

height of Gore is almost reached: Hee-Jin, the female character, pushes fishhooks into her vagina. Hyun-Shik, the man she loves, has already attempted earlier to kill himself by swallowing some.

Every object is thus double-edged, and can be diverted to more painful issues. The bow is, at the same time, a musical instrument and a death device, even if the old man only uses it in a dissuasive way. He merely sharpens his arrows to keep away the pretenders, but never, in *The Bow*, do those blades take someone's life.

Yet Kim Ki-duk never hesitates playing with the level of pain tolerance of the spectator: cannibalism, zoophilia, immolation by fire, eye-gouging (*Address Unknown*), the trade of corpses in *Crocodile* are some of the experiences and adventures of the extreme. In some scenes of *The Isle*, there is the possibility for latent scatology. In *The Bow* there is the possibility of urolagnia as well as an incest issue. Teenage prostitution brushes with the idea of paedophilia in *Samarian Girl*. One witnesses several rapes and abortions worthy of the butcher's. In *Address Unknown*, dogs are tortured for gastronomic purposes while, in the same film, a young woman has a zoophilic relationship with her pet dog.

Also in that same film, a son regularly tortures his mother. That American-Korean boy, named Chang-guk, goes as far as cutting the breast of the woman who proves he is mixed race before killing himself. The mother, mortified by her child's death, sinks into a kind of necrophilic cannibalism. She chews on her son's dead flesh, as if to swallow her own tragedy and return it to nothingness. To go back in time and erase the scars. To digest then get rid of the traces of what she considers a mistake and for which she has already paid a high price: giving birth to a child conceived with the American enemy.

Human bestiary: Animals and Animosity

If Kim Ki-duk's characters are mute, it's perhaps because violence is often muted. But above all it's because the director believes more in acts than in spoken words. And as autistic as those characters might be, their silence brings us closer to our animal side. In *3-iron*, the mute Sun-houa, abused by her husband, is much more chatty than Tae-suk, who discreetly enters people's homes. It is the animosity and the bestiality of human beings which can be read in those characters. Hang-gi, the male character in *Bad Guy* stares at Sun-hwa with predatory eyes the second he sees her. Then he violates her with a long kiss, as if to allow his animal impulses to speak. Not one word is exchanged between them before the end of the film. The cause of Hang-gi's mutism is to be found in the scar he has on his neck: it allows us to imagine several possibilities, all dramatic, of course. One thinks first about a settling of scores between pimps which would have deprived him forever of his voice. But, in another film, *Real Fiction*, one of the protagonists with the same scar on his neck, confides that he has been the victim of tortures inflicted by the marines during his stay in a military camp.

And like small animals, human beings have as much survival instinct for they are inhabited by a primitive rage. However, from anthropology to anthropomorphism, men's fate is not so different from the fate of the small animals that the little boy torments for his own entertainment in *Spring, Summer, Fall, Winter... and Spring*. The same thing goes for that tiny tortoise which launches into crossing the motorway during the credits in *Birdcage Inn*. It has more chance to survive than the dogs hunted and beaten by Eye of Dog, the canine butcher in *Address Unknown*. Why are they violently treated before being put to death? So that their flesh becomes more tender, and thus, more savoury. They wait for the end of the Calvary with wisdom and humanity. Besides, Eye of Dog, doesn't feel any different from them, neither for his look of dominant male amongst a pack of dogs, nor when he creeps into their cage, even less when he replaces them on the gallows at the end of the film. They suffer their fate and burden as on the Way of the Cross. Like those two other dogs joined together like Siamese twins in the same film: they have remained stuck together after coitus, both trying to go off in the opposite direction. Little chance of survival for all those fragile creatures, but they have at least the merit of giving human beings some lessons in life. Like them, the man usually feels trapped by his sexual needs.

The female animal: a many-faced creature

To persevere on that anthropomorphic line, one notices the title of the film *Birdcage Inn*, in which Kim Ki-duk brings together two young women of incompatible moods in the same inn, looking slightly like two kinds of birds. As in *The Bow* in its pure fashion, where two real hens symbolize marriage, or in *Bad Guy* in its vulgar version, where the image of the poultry comes to mind with the prostitutes, light, bouncing and sometimes feathered, suddenly start to argue violently over their clients. But in Kim Ki-duk's films, the woman who is predominant is especially beautiful and fluid, as if originating from the aquatic world. As long as the fisherman do not pull her out of her natural environment, she reigns on the waters, above and below. Thus it is often in the shape of a fish that she appears to us. But the fisherman never have the best destinies in store for her. Electrocuted, asphyxiated, tortured, reduced to a sashimi state... fish reflect the fate reserved for women, in the proper as well as the figurative sense. In spite of that, they have a survival instinct. Like that mute and bewildered carp faced with cutting up, and which, still alive by god knows what

36 ▶ 37 ▶

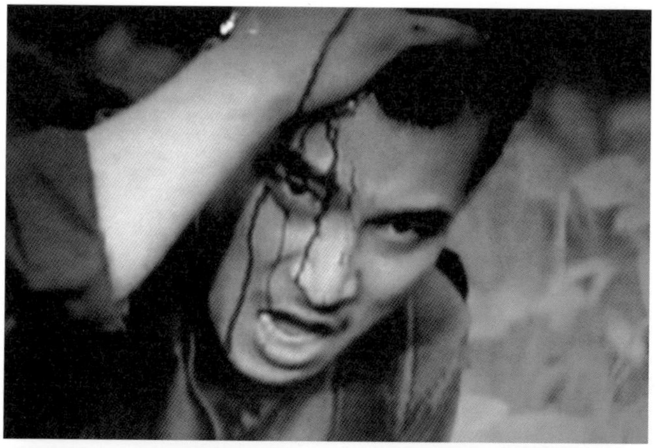

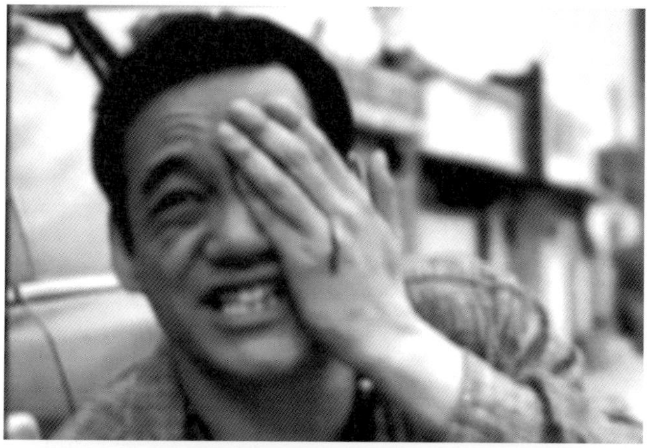

38 ▶ 39 ▶

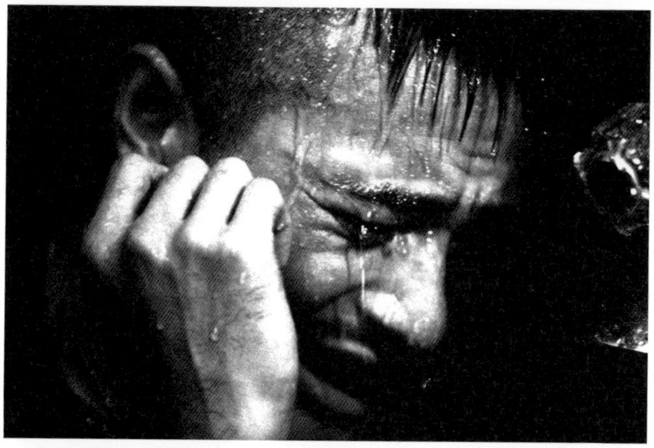

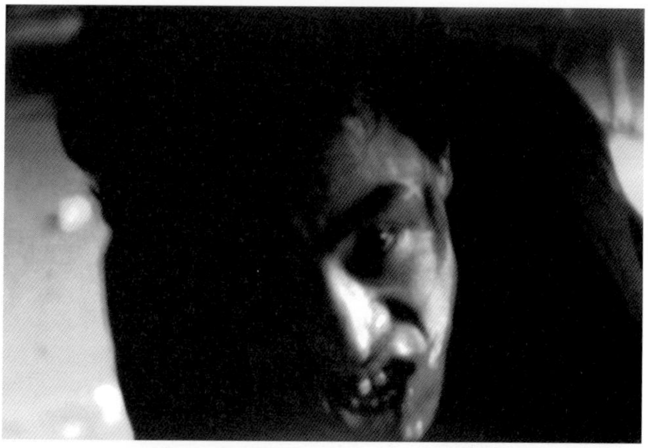

40 ▶ 41 ▶

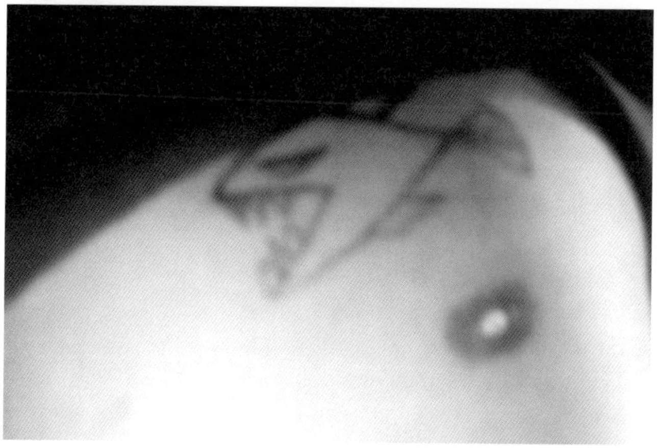

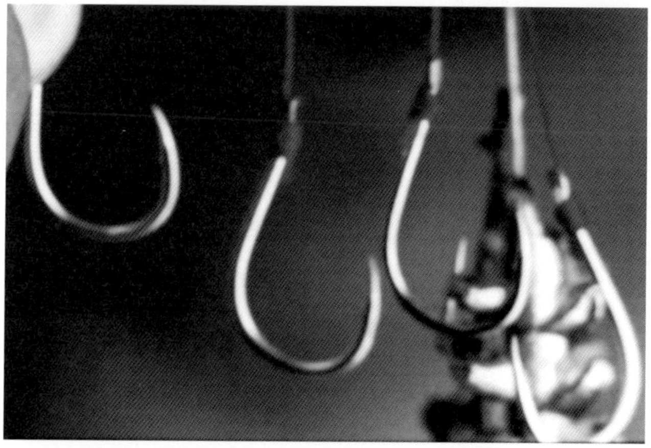

42 ▶ 43 ▶

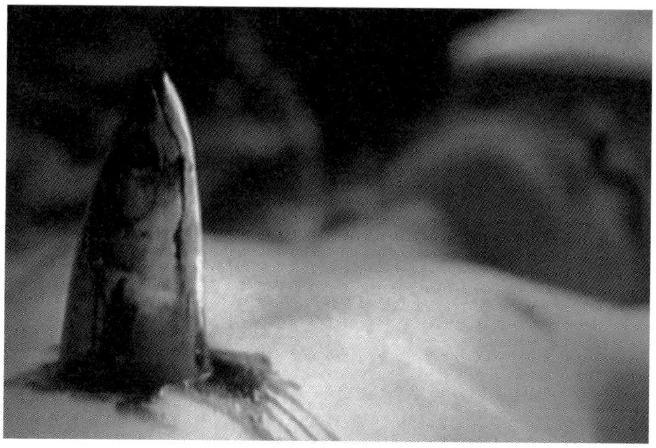

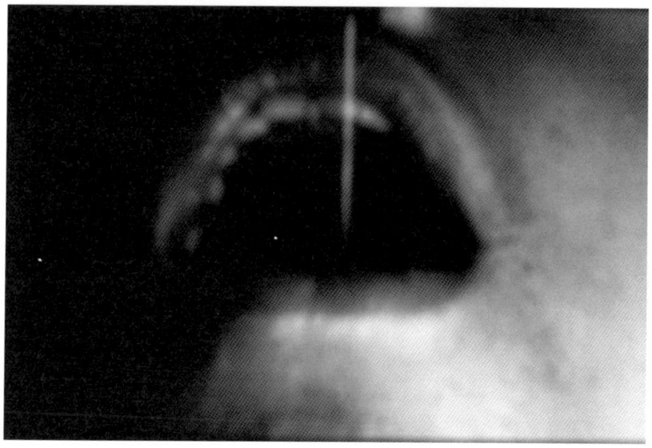

miracle, is returned to the water to calmly go on its way. In *The Isle*, the prostitute who pays a visit to Huyn-Shik has no such luck. She is a foolhardy fish that has started to spawn in a lake inhabited by another fish. Realizing that she won't be able to undo the shackles fixed by the mistress of the place and that escape will be a slow death in the open air, she chooses to tumble into the water of the lake and drown. The aquatic world contains creatures with no compassion for one another.

Fish and fishermen watch each other closely, without understanding each other too well, through the partition walls which could be those of a fish tank, or something similar: behind the peep-show booth in *Wild Animals*, or through the two-way mirror in *Bad Guy*... until Hang-gi tries to make contact with Kim Sun-hwa by the light of his lighter, for example. And since men and women feed on some kind of dependency towards each other, it is Kim Sun-hwa who breaks the glass to come closer to Hang-gi. In *Coast Guard*, Mee-Young, whose fisherman fiance has been killed while they were making love, becomes mad: she walks a fish on a lead. One sacrificed. As if it was her own asphyxiated life which was teetering like that, in the open air, hanging on the end of a string.

But much more than a mere creature, one realizes that the woman is an island, as in the film bearing the same title. She is a territory which holds back the men in captivity thanks to the powers of her sex. And if the woman is an island, she is also a fertile ground that falls pregnant and aborts with the greatest suffering: Mee-Young having slept with most of the soldiers of the camp in *Coast Guard*, and, covered in blood after her unbearable abortion, seeks refuge into a fish tank to soothe herself.

Among fishermen, since the beginning of time, numerous superstitions keep alive the fear of a female presence on boats. Those sinners are supposed to be synonymous with calamity. In Kim Ki-duk's films, the fishermen have no fear of swallowing fishhooks and desire women passionately.

The woman here is a kind of goddess, an enigmatic creature, if not a fantastic and unreal being who doesn't hesitate from swimming in troubled water, in the muddy and nocturnal depths of *The Isle*, for example. She is a seacow, perhaps even a mermaid, a siren.

And like Adam and Eve in Paradise, it is a woman who creates trouble in the regular rhythm of the seasons in *Spring, Summer, Fall, Winter... and Spring*: she arrives and arouses the sexuality of an innocent young man. In *3-iron*, the only female presence doesn't bring luck to Tae-suk, but rapidly sends him to prison.

A she-devil in spite of herself, at best the woman is a temptress who arouses man's desire, at worst, a prostitute. But whatever she is, whether she is paid or not for her services, the woman is venal and perverse by nature, and that as soon as she is a child, as the teenagers in *Samaritan Girl* prove. Eun-ok, the one-eyed teenager in *Address Unknown*, ends by denying the amorous feeling she has for Jihum, in order to start a relationship with the GI: in reality, she has deliberately chosen to sell herself in order to be able to afford a new eye. This transaction then seems natural, like to prostitute oneself occasionally, as Hee-Jin, the heroine of *The Isle*, does.

And each time, what women are blamed for is the commotion provoked in the man, which pushes him generally first to possessiveness, then to crime. For women in Kim Ki-duk's films are brutalized, beaten, raped, forced into prostitution... but deep inside, they are as generous as a Geisha, and that, whatever their age. To surrender the rights on her body doesn't always depend on a contract to which one submits, forced and compelled, as in *Bad Guy*. The woman in Kim Ki-duk's films is like Vasumitra, that Indian prostitute with an indelible smile who gives her body with infinite pleasure as an offering to her joyful clients. The teenage girl in *Samaritan Girl* uses her as a model. "She showed them maternal love. Men are like babies when they have sex," she declares, dream-like, establishing an obvious connection between love and prostitution. As for the man, he is more or less pushed into the role of pimp and expects the woman to satisfy him whenever he needs to be. At the same time, he finds it difficult to accept the idea that she doesn't sell her body... as is the case for the brother of Eun-ok in *Address Unknown*, for example. And in that stratagem, the spectator is as much a voyeur as an accomplice.

Not easy for each of the protagonists to go beyond their true nature. Their relationship is fatal, and that finds its full meaning when the sexual act and the ecstasy become the precise moment when one of the couple in *Coast Guard* is accidentally killed. Young-kil is shot by accident in the throes of love-making, when he is between the thighs of his beloved. The fisherman is shot like game by the soldier Kang. That death in the midst of love-making which is also the "little death", the metaphor for sexual orgasm, is a recurrent motif in Kim Ki-duk's cinema. It is a dramatized death.

Choreographed death: from reality to "the water-beyond"

Like love-making, death is choreographed as often as possible. One never dies too quickly or too easily in Kim Ki-duk's films, one lingers in that in-between. Death is a liberation one has to deserve. The hero in *Bad Guy* bleeds all the time, one think he's dead several times and each time he rises from the ashes with the same fervour. The discreet suicide of the prostitute in *Birdcage Inn* is a failure: she is saved by her arch enemy while traces of her blood are discreetly absorbed by toilet paper. In *The Bow* the old man tries to strangle himself with the rope of the boat in which his beloved sails away. The mixed race guy in *Address Unknown* inflicts a slow and exemplary death on his step-father, Eye of Dog. It's a death that seems to have been premeditated for a long while. He himself will die in a spectacular way, after falling from his moped: he is found with his head planted in the ice, his two legs pointing towards the sky. His mother will have to create a circle of fire around him to free his corpse from its prison of ice and retrieve him. One imagines she wants to give him a worthy burial: in fact, it is her own body which becomes her son's tomb, for she begins to ingest him.

Beyond those set-up killings, some sequences create confusion between reality and fantasy. In *Coast Guard*, a character in camouflage merges with the night. He is like a creature hiding in the shadow, spying on the soldiers like a hunter on the look out for game. As for Tae-suk, the male character in *3-iron,* he is a ghostly presence who, at the end of the film, seems to have acquired the gift of invisibility. That passing-through-walls seems to have found a solution to love: to live in his beloved's shadow, in the proper as well as the figurative sense. Kim Ki-duk's films often meet a fantastico-mystical outcome. Each ending is open to a variety of possible interpretations.

Where to find the cosmic balance which would pacify the relationship between men and women? The Brahmanic mythology, ever-present in Korea, offers perhaps an identity to that mythic creature that is the woman in Kim Ki-duk's cinema. One thinks about the spouse of Shiva, Mahadavi, the goddess with a thousand faces and a thousand names. She is the Earth-Mother, fertile and multiple who gathers in her all the others and thus absorbs all their qualities and characteristics. She is, for example, Durga the inaccessible, who fights the demons who haunt the men, or else Minakshi, a warrior and conqueror of the world, with fish eyes, whom one thinks about with the heroine of *The Bow*, who, brought by the water, seduces all the fishermen, including her adoptive father, who is the first to want to marry her as soon as possible. The faithful spouse of Shiva, she is in harmony with him. He has a cobra around his neck, carries a trident and holds in his hand a small percussive instrument. His emblem is the lingam, a phallus. Once again, one thinks about *The Bow*, the film, but also the instrument with a double function which is the bow and which dominates that narrative. The bow is here a symbol of male power. It is an object the old man brandishes proudly in his beloved's direction as she pushes him away. He carries on regardless, stretching his bow to prove his virility and vigour. The bow in the film is at the same time a death device, a tool to predict the future and a very delicate musical instrument. It is both creation and destruction, like Shiva the cosmic dancer who shares with the character of the old man in *The Bow* a quasi-cosmic energy as well as harmony. He can disappear into the water's depths after his wedding and give himself to death, and the pleasure of his young wife becomes visible by manifesting itself in blood. The old man has come back from the "beyond" to deflower his beautiful virgin bride in total quiet.

One reaches there a "beyond" (au-delà), or, more appropriately, a "water-beyond" (eau-delà), since it's in water that human beings continually find some comfort. Water unifies, regenerates, pacifies. Kim Ki-duk's characters bathe in the sea, meditate under the rain or create from bath rituals a means of communication between themselves, as in *The Bow* or *Samaritan Girl*. It is a maternal sea which is something like amniotic fluid. A fluid world, magical and everlasting.

The geography of Korea, its insularity, has something to do with the appeasement generally offered by the aquatic world in Kim Ki-duk's films. Moreover, the sea even unifies couples as improbable as the Democratic People's Republic of Korea, the communist regime of North Korea, and South Korea, whose political system is unitary. Exactly like the two Korean immigrants who enter into a contract in *Wild Animals*: Blue Ocean, the artist, originates from the South, and Red Mountain, the Martial Arts specialist, from the North. Korea is at the same time both one and divided. It is at the heart of the tensions, it makes unification difficult but not impossible.

The red of the Communism of the Democratic People's Republic, and the blue which represents South Korea… And also the red of blood and the blue of the water and seas which border that Asian peninsula… that is what one remembers of the tense world created by Kim Ki-duk. A blue world like the negative cosmic forces of the Yin, and a red world like the positive cosmic forces of the Yang, two opposed entities which interlace in the middle of the Korean flag. A symbol itself surrounded with the four elements in the four corners of the flag: water opposed to fire, and earth to sky. In his films, Kim Ki-duk tends towards a harmony which plays with opposites. Between opposition and balance, between positive and negative energies, between men and women, it is the immutable order of the world that Kim Ki-duk depicts through his work.

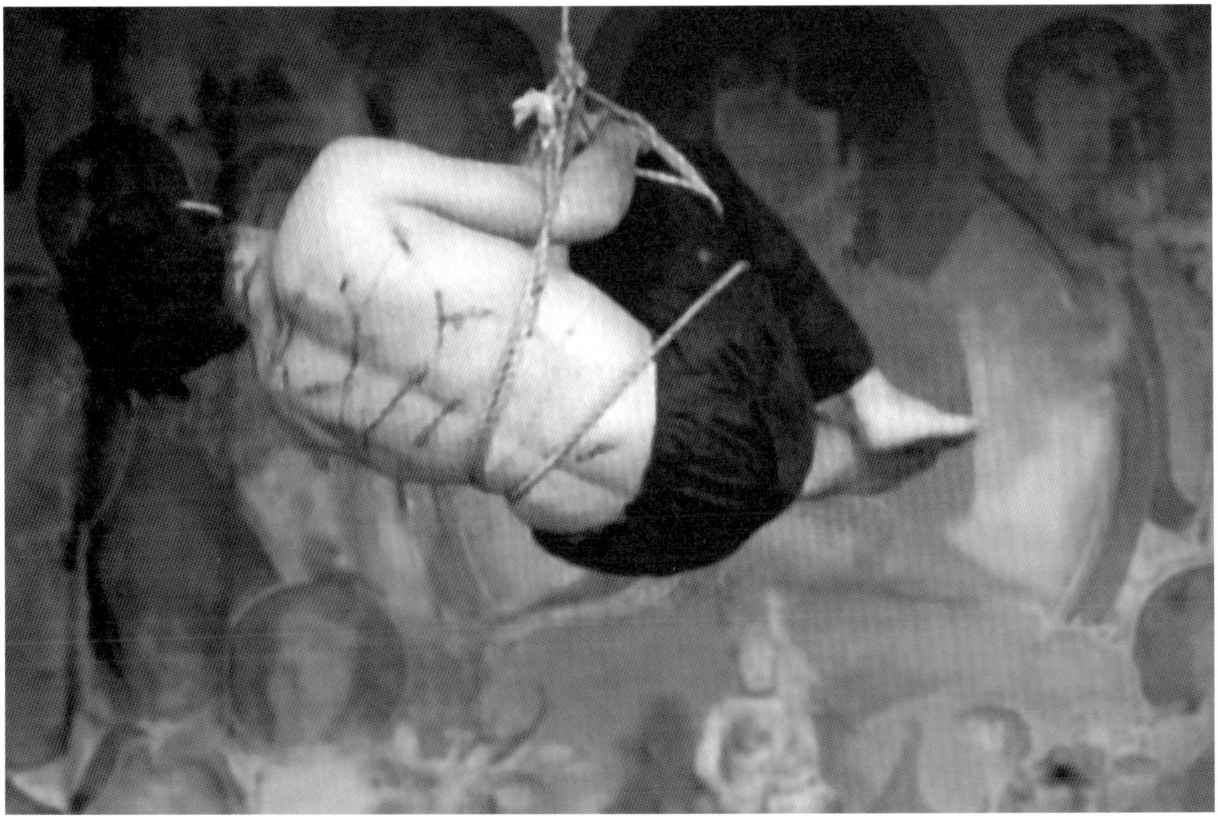

◄44

45 ▼

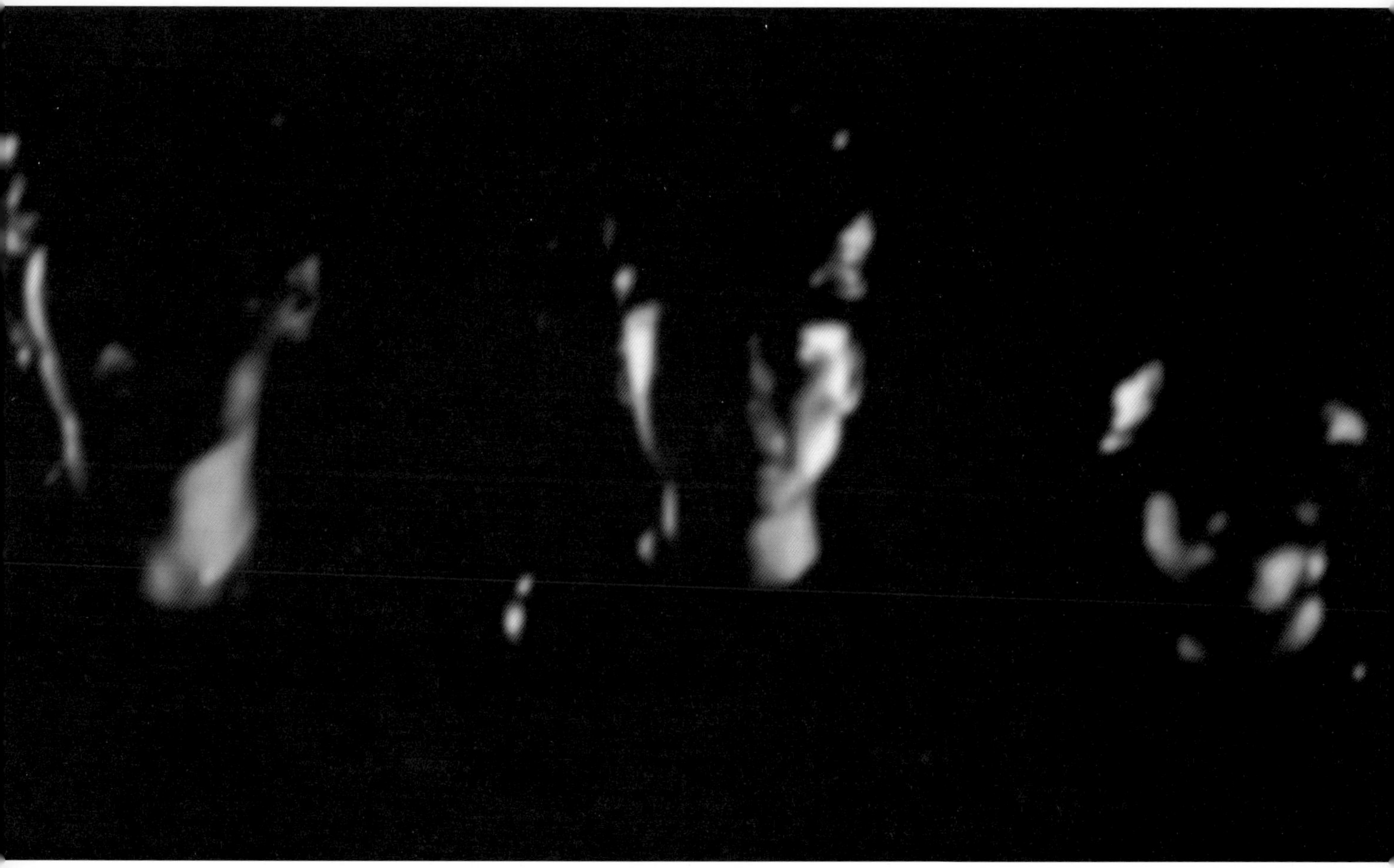

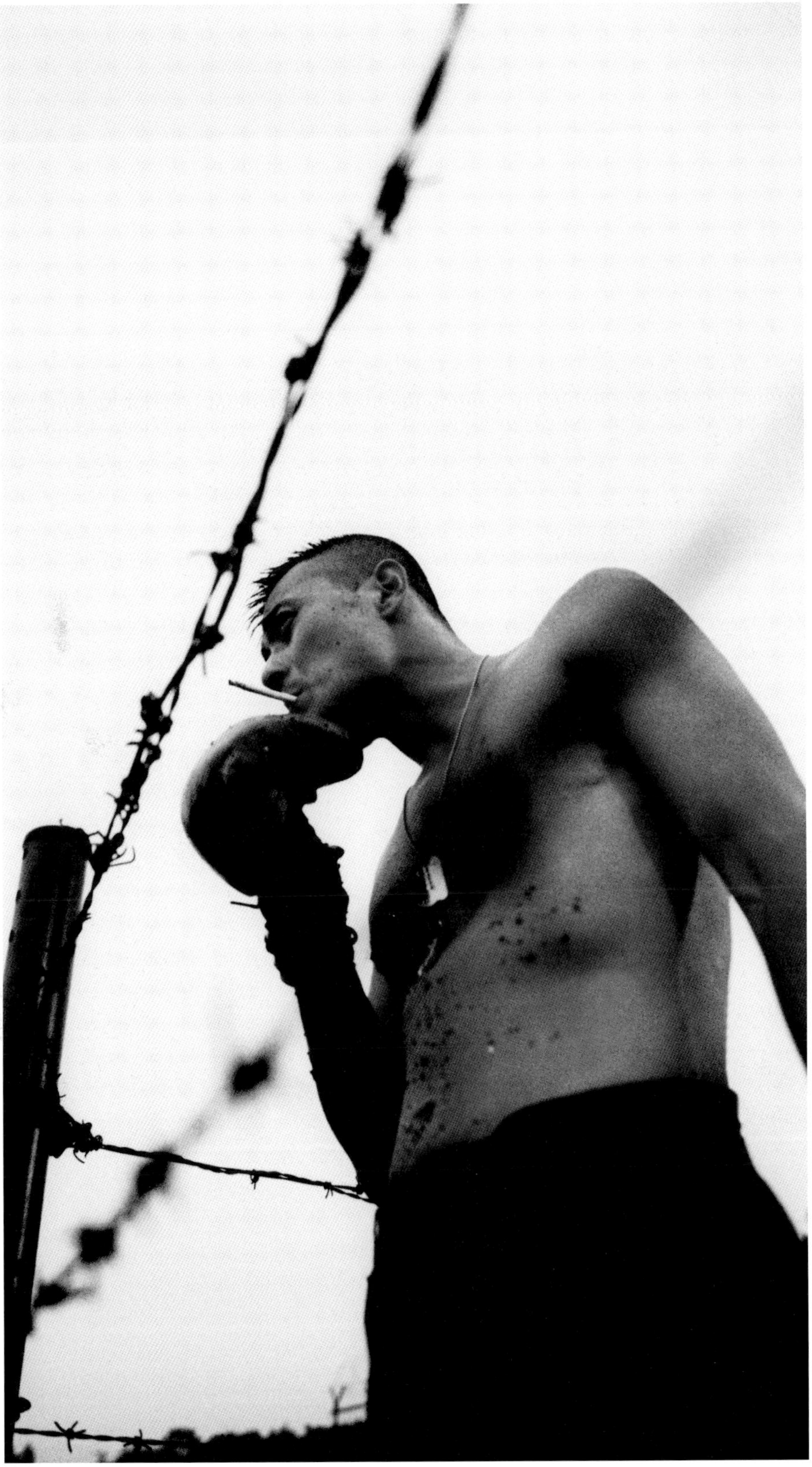

◄46

47 ▶

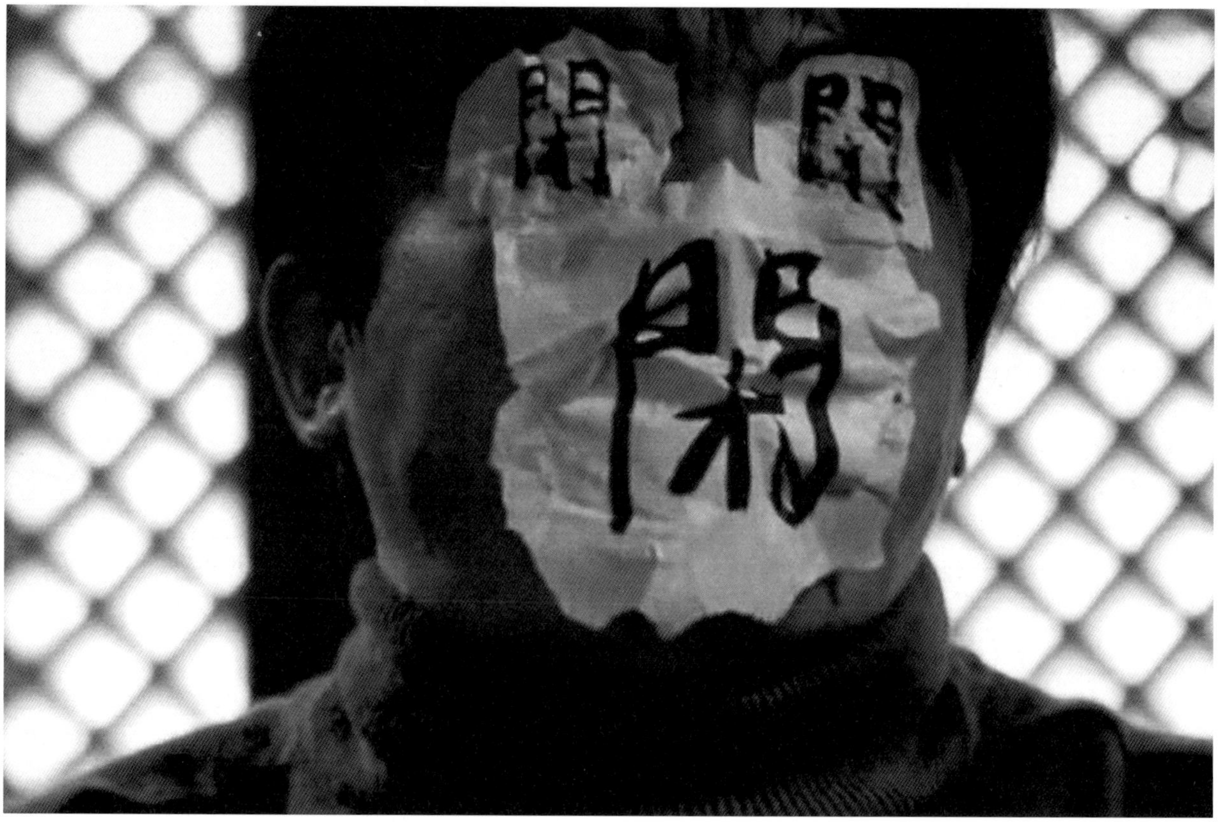

SPOKEN WORDS IN SUSPENSE

"What's requisite for communication is a defect or 'fault'. Communication enters like death through a chink in the armour. What's required is an overlapping of two lacerations, mine, yours."

Georges Bataille, *Guilty*.

Cruel game

In *Spring, Summer, Fall, Winter... and Spring*, the old monk's disciple, still a child, tortures various animals (a fish, a frog and a snake) by attaching a stone to each. For him it is just a game, a game children play. Innocence is cruel for it has no idea of the harm it does, and for innocence nothing ever really happens. The only way to become aware of what is happening is to suffer oneself. That is the reason why the old monk ties a stone to the child. Then and only then does he perceive the other side of innocence, the cruelty which is its price.

That is the first violence, not only unable to account for itself, to justify itself, but even deprived of hatred, or affect, and only practised through playing a game. And that game, paradoxically, has no less terrible effects: if what happens as a game doesn't really happen, or doesn't happen *for real*, the damage done is irreparable: two of the animals in *Spring...* die from that cruelty. In the same way, the one-eyed girl in *Address Unknown* has lost her eye for no reason: there is no compensation for that loss, no meaning, for, as her brother who has deprived her of it, says, "it was just a game!" It didn't really happen, but in reality it did, irreversibly. It was not for real, but the girl has really lost her eye. Things are not taken seriously, lives have no meaning, nothing echoes their misery, nothing justifies them, however, they happen, irreparably.

That is why those things, the death of the animals, the eye of the girl remain in suspense, demanding atonement: for as they are they envelop the world, in the shape of an account to settle, with a halo of absurdity. That cruelty is not answerable for itself: while one cannot avoid questioning the meaning, it remains in excess in relation to every possible meaning, it remains purely gratuitous. For it is not only violence, an obsessive theme in Kim Ki-duk's films, which is gratuitous: it is, even more so, the gratuitousness of what is happening which in itself is violent. Life never answers the call for meaning, it doesn't hold onto the promise for meaning that language formulates. Life remains in suspense, or the language, like a promise of meaning, has too much of it.

That is what another woman in *Address Unknown* experiences in a terrible way: her life is spent writing to an American soldier whose child she has, letters which invariably come back. *Absurdum*: literally what makes a dull sound when one bashes it, what doesn't respond. The film unfolds in the emptiness of the wait caused by that address without a recipient, that *sign too many* which has no meaning for anybody. What the letter says is not important: a simple declaration of existence, but without a recipient – of an absurd existence thus, unnecessarily admitting its own absurdity, exposing itself unnecessarily to that deadly blow that is silence, and to the unbearable indifference of things. That is the very first violence, that from which all the others flow: language, through which the character risks asking for meaning, through which the character questions the meaning, remains in suspense. Language, which formulates those promises, remains as surplus in a world devoid of meaning. A violence without blows which is that of life itself.

It is that first insult, the gratuitous violence which constitutes the irrational reason for all violence. It is in response to that violence, in response to the absence of response, that the characters become tough, withdraw, close up from each other. Overwhelmed by their passions, their anger, their desire, they become the *very face* of passion, anger, and desire. Like that high angle shot in *The Bow* in which the girl locked-up, motionless on the cabin bed, looks at the camera, totally incensed. Communication is no longer possible between those hardened people. Individualities are opaque, almost impossible to bend. Kim Ki-duk doesn't hide the difficulty he has in comprehending violence, but he observes the human monoliths with enough care to be able to go back to that first wound, that letter without recipient, that scream which always returns. That is where we take it from, and the director doesn't give to any facility on the subject: if the blocks of hatred, desire, egotism (above all in his first films) are truly a symbolizing of undiluted passions, it is because, in real life, the system of symbols doesn't work. The characters are the symbols of the impossibility of symbolizing. They appear so crudely only on the background of the impossibility of language itself: impossibility, consequently, of adapting to the social world, of polishing one's vices, of softening them through relationships with fellow humans. People don't talk to each other in Kim Ki-duk's films, people hit each other. Relationships are always frontal, direct, decoded, never mediated through language which would neutralize the violence and allow individualities to meet in the neutrality of a shared space. The differences experienced by the social body, are not differences which are relative, susceptible to find in conversation or negotiation, a reasoned resolution; they are absolute differences, with no possible agreement, with no possible communication, which will only be settled through sacrifice, madness or death.

The absolute difference

One is tempted to find, in the political reality of Korea, a true expression of that violence. For the division of the country, as *Coast Guard* bears witness, is a material and not a symbolic division, marked by a very real fence which cuts into the body of Korea itself: nothing goes through, nothing is exchanged, no trade, no dialogue. That division between North and South operates abroad too; in *Wild Animals*, which is set in France, the two Koreans who meet reproduce it in their relationship. As if that first division contributed to making them strangers to themselves, as if the violence of the cut deprived them of the possibility to dominate the violence in themselves. And since Korean language is not the language of a country at peace with itself, but that which, in spite of themselves, the brother-enemies share; since it is not, in Korea itself, that which dresses the wounds, resolves the conflicts, since it cannot do anything faced by that laceration which it has however the inclination not so much to restore as to appease (bringing with it not harmony but at least a possibility of understanding which, in each particular conflict, generates the hope for an agreement); since, in the end, that shared meaning which is the language common to both states, doesn't find any correspondence in the reality, the meaning itself ends up being discredited. The language is now subordinate to that violence it was supposed to put an end to: those who, in *Wild Animals* or in *Address Unknown,* play the baddies, only utter the typical statements which characterize nastiness, as the liars can no longer do anything but lie, and nobody really takes words seriously. Language cannot set itself free, cannot exist for itself, nor can it generate its most characteristic power, which is a fragile agreement between human fellows, miraculously saved from all violence. Language remains caught in the monoliths of nastiness, violence and despair. Contracts are passed, though, but one knows immediately that they won't be honoured, that the

48 ►

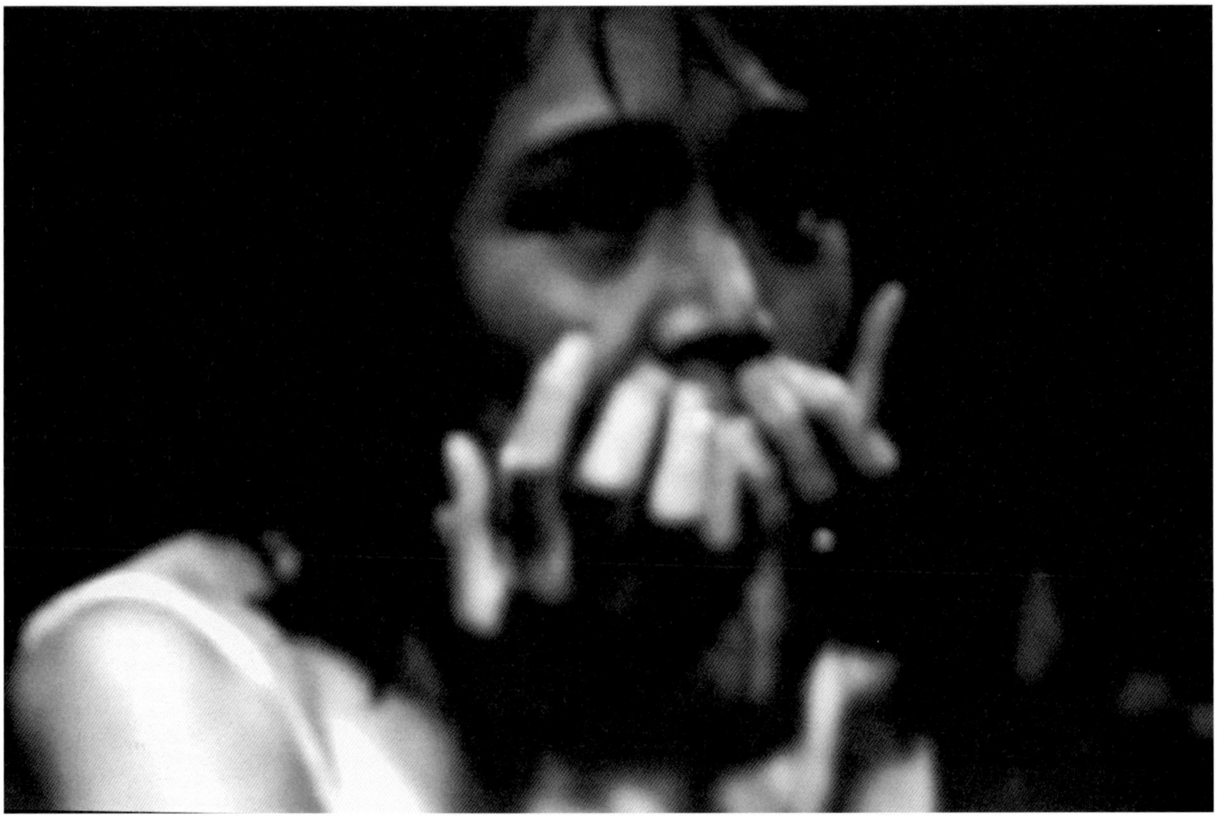

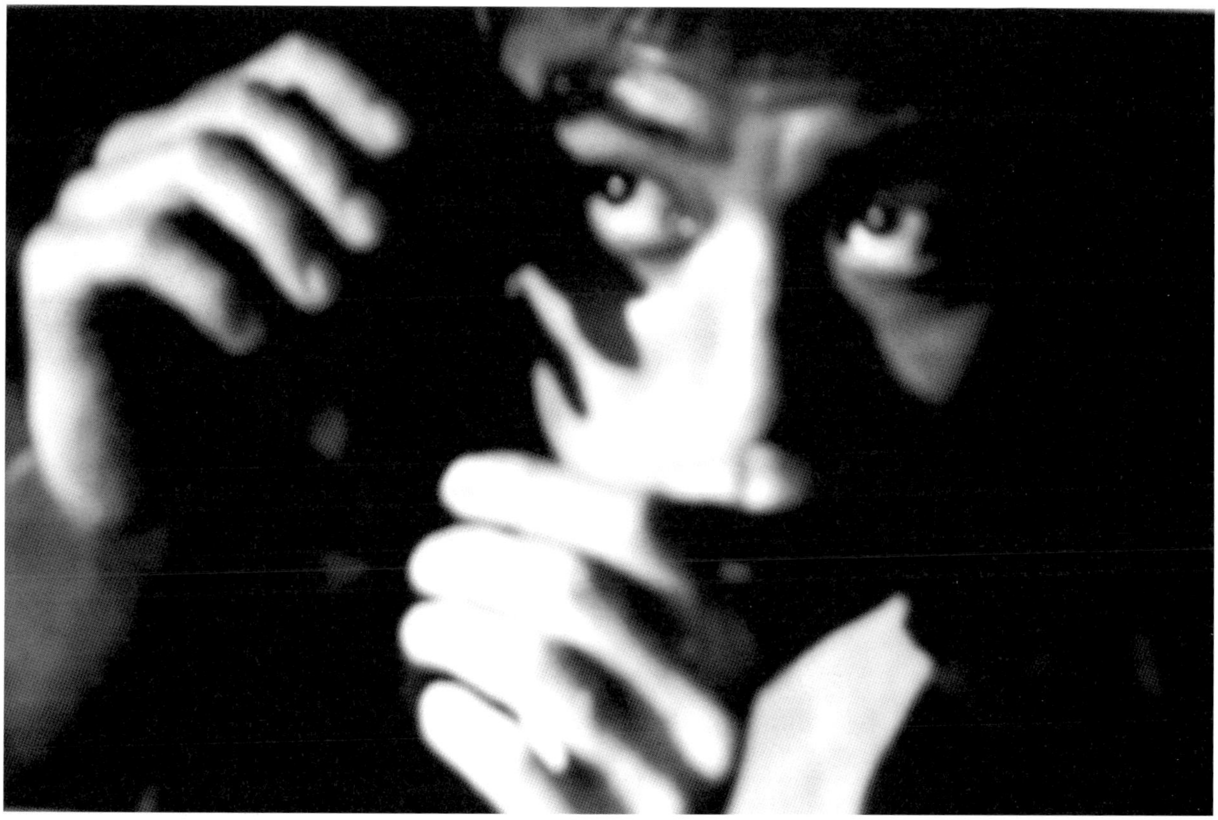

◀ 49

contracts are a deception, and that only relationships of power exist: imitation or similacrum of words rather than real words.

However, Korea's division is only a motif, the symbol of a division one finds under a multitude of forms. If there is anything resembling social criticism in Kim Ki-duk's cinema, it is not the criticism of such or such society, but rather the final report on social aporia. The report on an absolute difference, never reducible to a punctual and finally soluable disagreement. The impropriety of the language and vanity of all words. For something, in social relationships, overflows from words, overflows from the negotiable, the irresolute nature of relationships – the pulsion of death. If, as usual, that something goes into profit and loss, into the shape of harmless individual neurosis most of the time, here, as in war situations, it siphons all languages and demonstrates its vanity. Language is not co-extensive to life, desire doesn't let itself be totally symbolized or spiritualized. So that no friendship even, as a miraculous formation of desire, is protected from a betrayal, from an excess, as one sees in *Wild Animals,* where, before changing his mind, the young lout from the South takes it upon himself to drown his northern friend.

The defeat of language leaves bare, open like a wound, the unbearableness of human relationships, the misery of solitudes in total desperation, mute monads whose paths never cross without a shock, without a clash, without the violence of the then-and-now which cannot be exceeded – of the non-mediatized by language. Without mediation, there is no common ground for two organized freedoms meeting, and each can only assert itself against the others, "a war of all against all". The meeting can only be a brutal confrontation, a relationship of power, non-communication and solitude.

The interval of time

Complex networks of fences, windows, obstacles everywhere prevent something from happening. But, like the zealous marksman in *Coast Guard*, one is craving for something to happen. One is on the look out, unceasingly, waiting for something – meaning – through the fissures of reality, to deliver us from the absurd and from solitude. The soldier who, sheltered in his sentry box, must prevent the intrusion of a spy coming from the North, plays his role with a zeal even more moving, even more raging and imperious for he has to

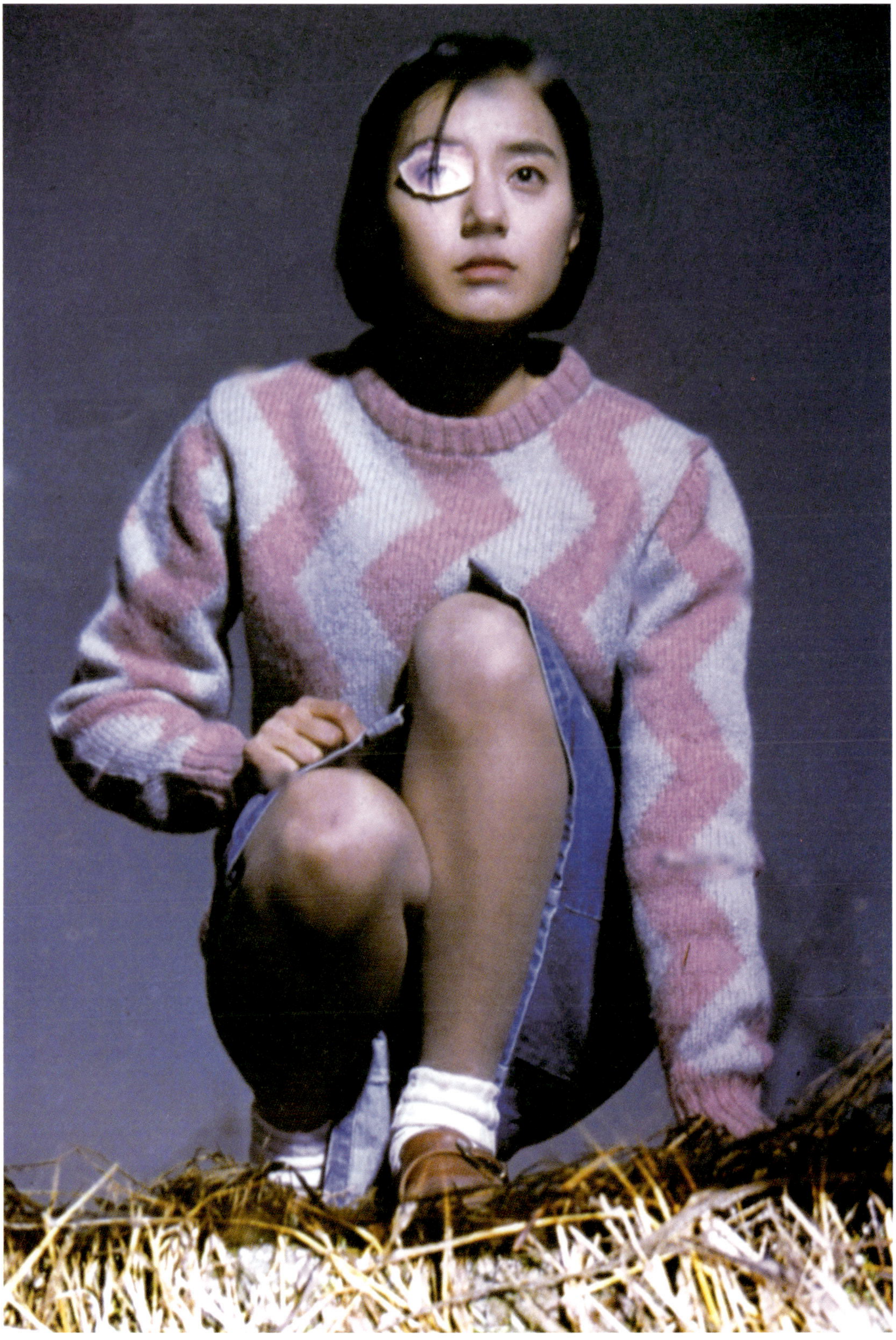

◀ 50

endure the jeers of the chorus, of the singularly ill-tempered inhabitants who look down on those useless soldiers, considering that vain discipline, all that arsenal, as a chimera. That world has stopped, those men are stuck: something has to move, it's a matter of breathing. The soldier is choking with the desire for something to happen, something which will give some meaning to his presence on that warless front, that front exposed to nothing, to nothingness. He is craving for something to circulate there where nothing can circulate, where nothing should circulate, and in that he shares the destiny of all those other characters who, in Kim Ki-duk's films, look through slats, two-way mirrors, windows, transparent plastic sheets, on the lookout for something… And when finally something does happen, it is obviously not what one was expecting. The shot misses its target (the potential and phantasmal spy) but brings down a young couple making love in no-man's land – at the same time the place where *nothing must happen* and that, alone amongst everything, where *something can happen*. There is, of course, love which circulates, but love is not considered as such. It is considered as something else: as the enemy so much fantasized upon, who alone, because of his arrival, can justify one taking up arms against each other. In the grid space of divisions which separate the bodies and install between them a forbidden zone, the lovers escape leads them to madness (that of the girl) and death (her young lover). The soldier receives a medal for his zeal, while an innocent one is dying: divisions made that absurdity possible. Decorated for having maintained at all costs the uselessness of that place, the nothingness of all events, and the brutal insignificance of reality.

Two contrary desires are at work: the desire for something to happen, and the exact opposite, the desire for nothing to happen. For all event is violent in a world without language. Eros and Thanatos oppose each other without mediation. However, there is no nostalgia in Kim Ki-duk's films for an eventual primitive harmony between human beings, a harmony from which we would have been separated because of false social divisions. The price for harmony is paid with the same destructive rage, as we see in *The Bow*. On a boat anchored far from the bank, an old man lives alone with the girl he's caring for, and whom he intends to marry on her seventeenth birthday. The bow, which he handles with skill and religiosity, exerts a double function: on the one hand to maintain, through the music he draws from it, the harmony of his small isolated world, on the other to repel the fishermen when their desire for the girl threatens the balance. He guarantees the fragile equilibrium of a territory stifling from exiguity, but musical, having found its place in the natural forces at work, and which can only be maintained through viciously rejecting the others. It is still in a way a fence. And it lasts until the day when, because of a young fisherman, desire makes their sweet eternity explode; in the girl's ears, the young man's walkman replaces the song of the bow. The old man's dream doesn't resist that intrusion of reality, that apparition from elsewhere. For innocence without cruelty is only a dream. Reality is the unpredictable violence of the event. And that is when confinement appears, for the spectator as well as for the girl, in its sinister reality: that of an old egotist who, despite all his love, prevents a young girl from living her life. That intrusion of desire is necessary to reveal the futility of the dream, its secret and deep violence. It is accompanied by a terrible refusal of time: that man, who thought he had cemented his eternity, is forced to feverishly tear the pages of his calendar to make the wedding happen quicker. But catastrophe has happened even quicker, the temporal tampering couldn't slow down the disarming speed of the event.

What prevents harmony is not the falsehood of divisions and the social codes, it's the plurality of desires and the speed of their intrusion. Kim Ki-duk doesn't look for any healing: the original wound is beyond healing, and the young disciple in *Spring, Summer, Fall, Winter…and Spring* "will," as his master says, "carry the stone in your heart for as long as you live". Paradise is nothing but a lie, except if it's earned in reality itself, which is rough and perverse. One cannot do without the difference. Nothing will happen in denial.

The endless running into debt

Because of that original wound, because of those "unkept promises", about which Kim Ki-duk repeats in his interviews that they are the origin of all violence, and about which one could also say that they are typical of the time, everybody withdraws into a stubborn silence. For everything is aggression. "The characters in my films are not mute," said Kim Ki-duk. "They just don't believe in verbal communication." It is not that they cannot speak, it's that they don't want to speak. They are not silent through inability to speak, but through the inability to believe in words. Phantasmal denial of the other which can only result, sadly, in exposing them even more to physical violence since, unless they isolate themselves physically from the world, they cannot avoid meeting others. Since no agreement can be reached, they have nothing to soften the blows, no symbolic equivalent, which would make

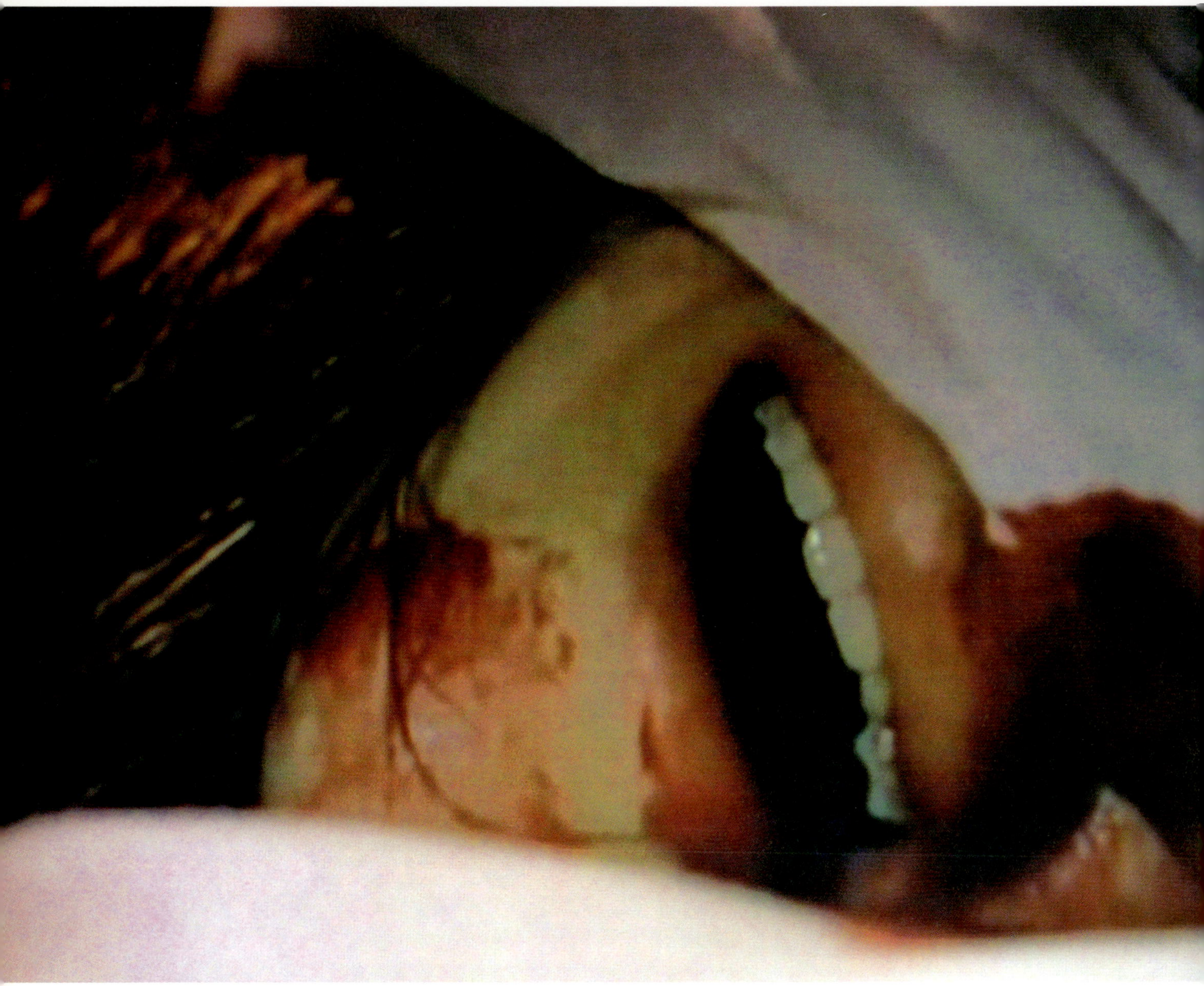

51 ▲

52 ▶

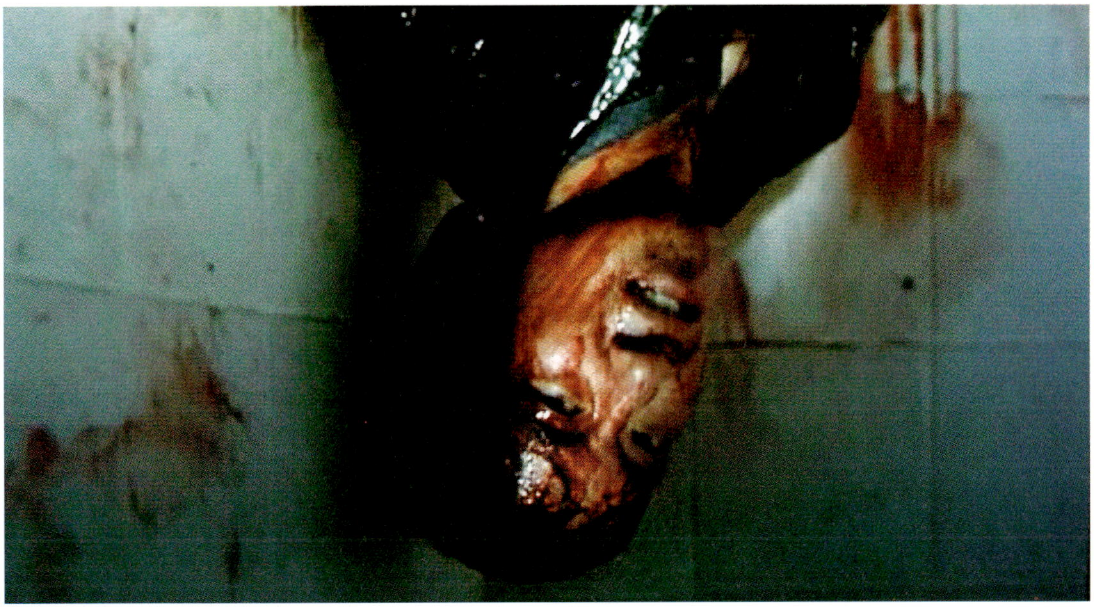

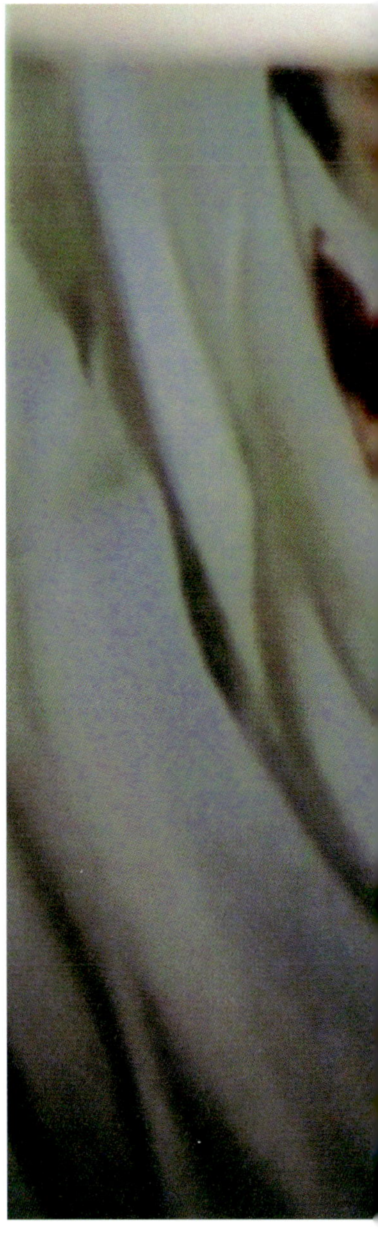

physical violence miss the bodies. For lack of language, for lack of civilized symbolizing of the relationships of power and affects, for lack of common law, accounts, whose balance is never nil, are settled by the bodies themselves, in exchanges of gunshots, wounds and blood. For something has to happen, because in the end, those solitudes *desire* each other, and that is the reason why they tear each other apart. Desire demands a relationship, even if that relationship is impossible. That is where the drama lies: the necessary is impossible.

The invisible cruelty of human relationships, the dominations and servitudes, normally concealed by their symbolic character, are expressed here in their real shape, material, physically mutilating and painful. I have power over you, so I beat you. I desire you so I enslave you, like Hang-gi in *Bad Guy* prostituting the girl he desires but doesn't touch. A character who chases out another, doesn't just say "Get lost!", he also has to half-knock him down, as in *Address Unknown* in which, almost each time two men, or a man and a woman, meet, one slaps the other most of the time. Each, in whatever group he/she is, ends up being the object of the gratuitous violence of the strongest and each passes on those blows to the weakest, down as far as women and animals who, at the bottom of the ladder, have no-one to beat in return and who die for the whole world, having absorbed all the social violence passed from hand to hand, like those unfortunate dogs hung up for their meat in *Address Unknown*, like that mutilated fish thrown back alive in the water in *The Isle*. It is towards women and animals that the flux of violence produced by social relationships are directed. It is women and animals who, through their powerlessness to pass them on, through their death, torture or servitude, allow the flux to be evacuated. Their annihilation is the price of survival of the whole.

For a world deprived of law is not, far from that, an original paradise for endless individual freedoms: it is rather the generalized running into debt of all beings towards all beings. Kim Ki-duk's characters are never free from one another. No mistake is even put right, no offence ever acquitted, the damage is irreversible. Law is generally what aims at making individual freedoms meet without friction, which thus ensure the coexistence of a plurality while at the same time redressing mutual attacks, by relativising the differences. But no law can produce a true harmony, or rather every law let out of its limits an irremediable, incodifiable violence, a mutual hatred, a fierce background of unsociability, of which wars are the breaking loose. The authority of the law demands as its condition not to be fixed, not to be solidified in the shape of a norm (that which should be), not to ever finish codifying the reality, and to produce symbolic equivalents allowing the reparation of the irreparable. Kim Ki-duk often insists on the extreme rigidity of the codes in force in Korea, especially in the register of sexuality. To be so far from reality empties the law of all authority. As if the law itself in its totality was invalidated because of this powerlessness to codify or recuperate the imperious sexual forces of work, forces which attract and set the bodies against each other.

Hang-gi, in *Bad Guy,* forces Sheon-Hwa to contract a debt. But immediately, what Sheon-Hwa owes Hang-gi is much more than money: Hang-gi has acquired an infinite right on her body. A hundred years of prostitution wouldn't be enough to reimburse it. And if by chance one succeeds in reimbursing a debt, it is at the cost of a mutilation: once again the story of the eye, in *Address Unknown*, is exemplary. Thanks to the soldier who tries to seduce her, the one-eyed girl has her eye treated, not knowing the debt she is contracting. Later, when the soldier, suddenly worried about the idea that she might forget him, wants to carve his name on her breast – for it is only like that, in wounding bodies, that one is sure in Kim Ki-duk's cinema that something has truly happened – he takes offence at her refusal: "After what I've done for you!" How to free oneself from such a debt? There is of course only one way: gouging her eye for the second time, symbolically giving back the eye he had taken care of.

The secret collusion

The relationships which one establishes, which inevitably end up being established between people are thus never "equitable" relationships. As the fugitive on *The Isle* only stays with the young prostitute for he is bound by a debt, it is again that first constraint which, in *Bad Guy,* binds Hang-gi to his young prisoner. At the beginning of the film, Hang-gi, who meets her in a park, doesn't bother seducing her. He doesn't have the slightest hope of making their two desires meet. So he kisses her by force, on the mouth, in the middle of a public garden. It is by no means a small violence. The mouth is perhaps the most intimate part, since it is from there that one speaks and, in Kim Ki-duk's films, from where several characters keep quiet. It is through the mouth that is spoken, on the contrary – by not speaking – the refusal of the world and the withdrawal. One accepts, ultimately, self-harm,

53 ▶
54 ▼

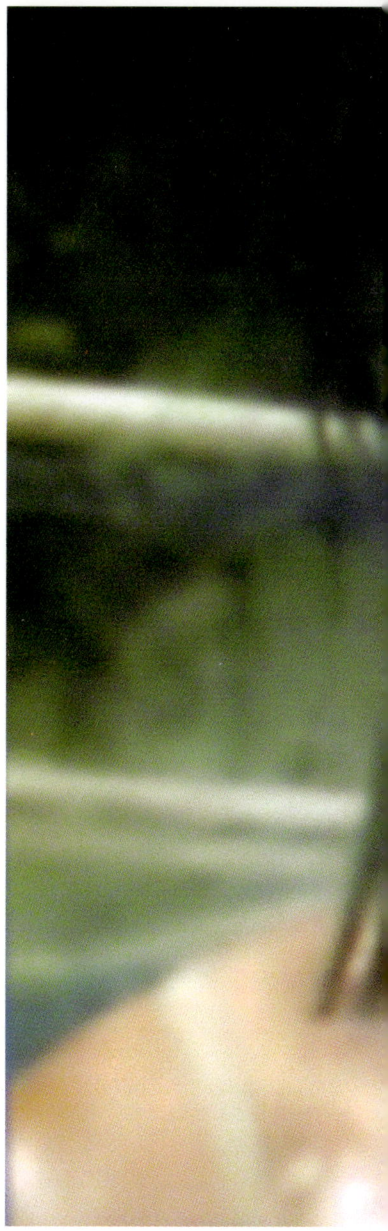

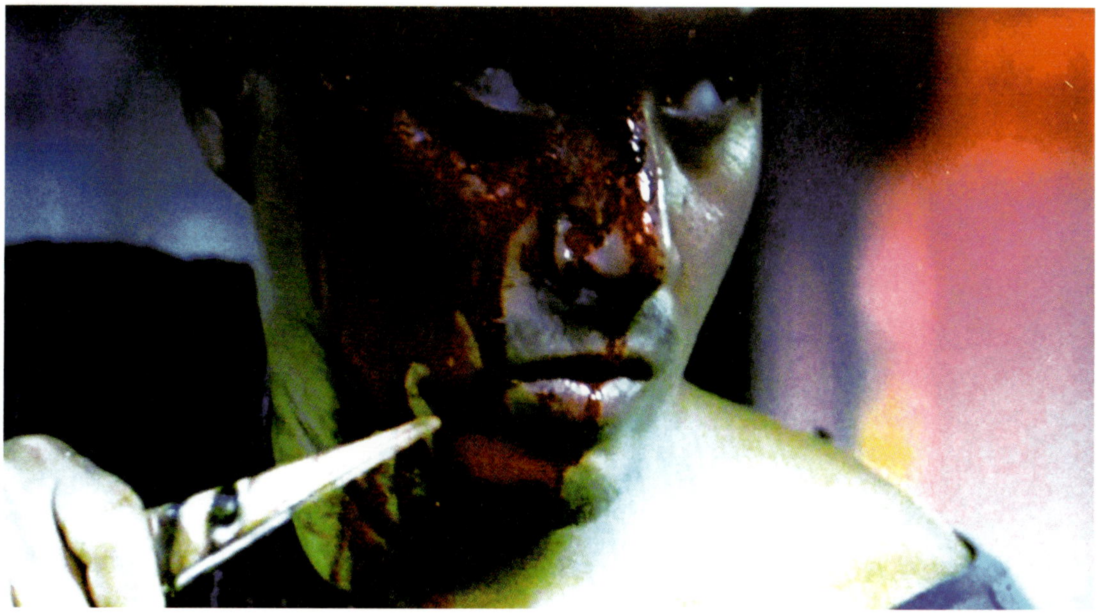

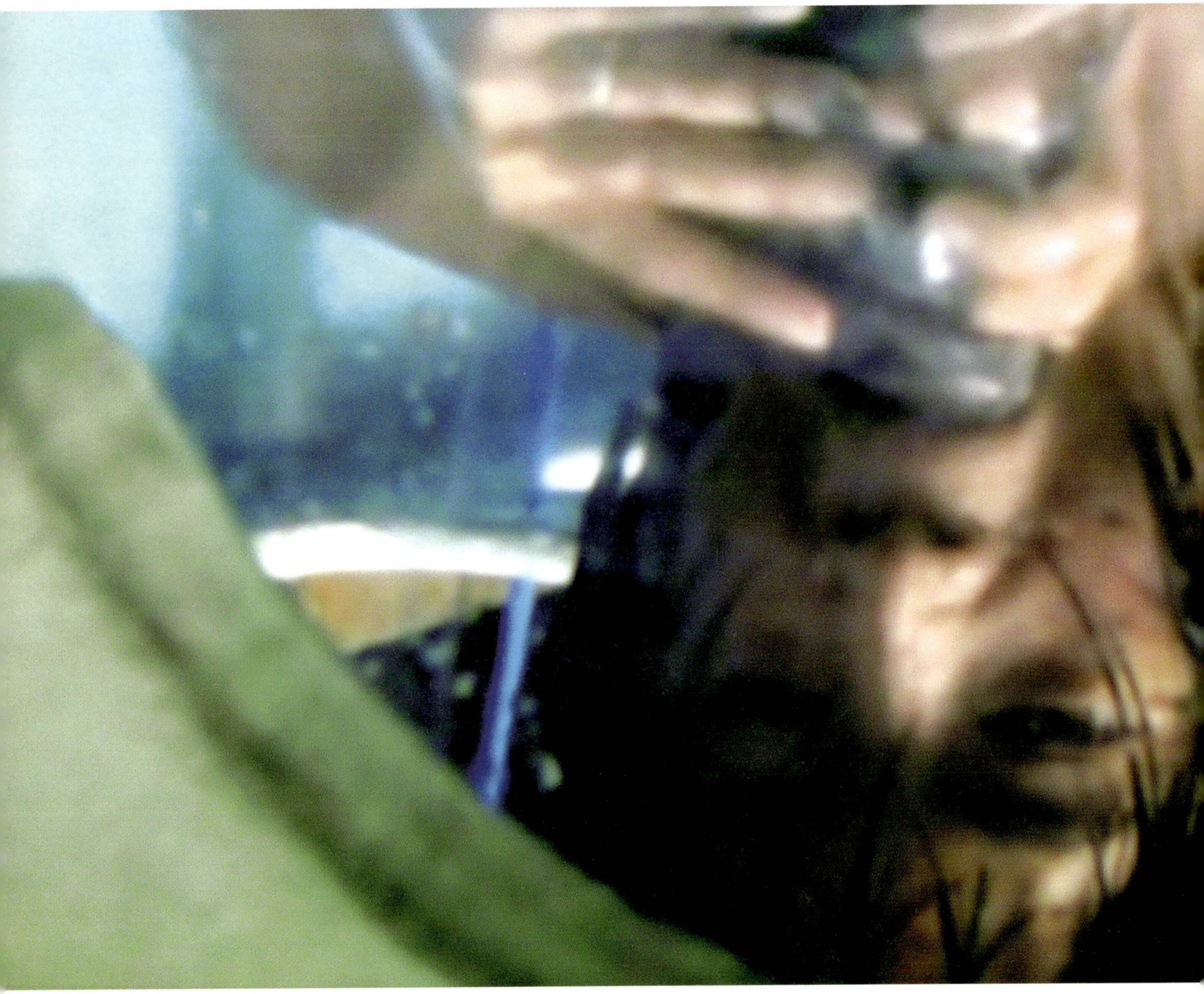

but not to speak, never. Rather to die. Hence the remarkable brutality of that gesture, its shamelessness, emphasized by the fact that it is accomplished in a public space where, in the Far East, one avoids kissing at all costs. The public slapping given by Sheon-Hwa doesn't leave them square and Hang-gi thinks he has permission, once the girl is his prisoner, to reimburse himself *ad infinitum*. But it is on that bizarre infinity, that infinite inequality, that, against all expectation, a compromise is found. First perceived in the image of her compassion, when she witnesses the beating up of Hang-gi by the local gang, then in the impossibility to escape when she has the chance.

"There is no sexual relationship," Lacan liked to stress. Sex is never a relationship between two subjects – neither reciprocity nor equality. It is, in *Bad Guy*, on the impossibility of the sexual relationship (on the possible impotency of the pimp) that a distanciated and silent relationship is built. From the girl the increasing consent of submission, if never really wholly consented; from Hang-gi a lessening of the brutal voyeurism, I mean a lessening of the hidden voyeurism. Hang-gi doesn't touch the girl: he spies inside the room where she receives her customers through a two-way mirror until the day he reveals himself with the flame of his lighter. Voyeurism is no longer a theft if the voyeur shows himself stealing. As for Sheon-Hwa, who first refused to prostitute herself, she becomes a real whore, adopts the necessary gestures, soliciting clients in the street, taking pleasure in the rivalry which, as is the usual practice when one takes on a profession, opposes her to the other girls. That voyeurism, and the complication of a relationship which one shouldn't reduce too quickly to a relationship between a rapist and his victim (in which one would be totally in the wrong, and the other totally innocent) is to be found in all of Kim Ki-duk's cinema: so, in *Address Unknown*, the draughtsman peeps at the young one-eyed woman, through the slats of a Venetian blind, being licked by her dog. When the girl notices, she's not offended, she never takes on the viewpoint of innocence. Instead, they look together at the pages of a porn magazine: "Have you ever seen me in those positions?" she asks. Or, in *Birdcage Inn*, a boy tapes the tenant's revels and masturbates while listening to them in his bed. But here the terms change, for the victim won't know anything about it. It is, in reality, the voyeur's sister (or should we rather say the listener?) who, for a moment indignant, will 'come', without her knowing, with the help of those recording.

Nobody is innocent and there is no pure and simple victim. That is merely an invention of the law, one of its categories which, in reality, in rape, voyeurism and prostitution, has the tendency to become blurred and consequently unsuitable for a moral or legal discourse. It becomes impossible thus to settle between the victim and his tormentor, some affects incessantly passing from one to the other. "To show the girls less like victims": that's how Kim Ki-duk answers those who accuse him of presenting a vile image of women (at least four of Kim Ki-duk's films have prostitution as central theme: *Birdcage Inn*, *The Isle*, *Bad Guy* and *Samaritan Girl)*. And inversely: to show men less like tormentors? For it is likely that domination leans even minutely, even unnoticed, on consent from the dominated. In the same way as profanation is not the destruction of mystery but, as Levinas said, one of the possible relationships to it, domination is not hatred for the dominated, but a possible relation to that other with whom I cannot speak, I cannot negotiate; altogether a relationship miraculously saved from the impossibility of all relationships. "The relationship between men and women is in itself a kind of prostitution," said the director, "even if no money changes hand." So it is a lie to pretend that a relationship between lovers is a relationship of equality. It is no more protected from relationships of power than from emotional debts and *advances* (to note both the economic and the amorous sense). The apparently purely commercial nature of the relationship between a pimp and his prostitute in reality conceals a real and unexpected meeting between two desires, however strangely adjusted, but necessary if one doesn't lean on a fantasy of ideal love, equal and pure. "When, for example, you offer a necklace to the girl you're going out with," Kim Ki-duk suggested, "and after that the girl sleeps with you, can't we consider it a form of prostitution?" *Bad Guy* shows that admirably: even once they are freed from their mutual hatred, Hang-gi and Sheon-Hwa don't change anything in their relationship: Hang-gi carries on selling her to strangers, entirely justified (for innocence has *to be earnt*) through Sheon-Hwa's consent. If, in reality, the flux of violence, insoluable residue of the unfulfillment of desires, passes through the social body, they don't pass without the equivalent flux of *jouissance*.

There is in that something highly Sadian, if not sadistic: "There is no man who doesn't want to be a despot when he has an erection," wrote Sade: desire is tyrannical and perverse (or to put it better, domineering and divine) and the idyllic representation of love a denial of reality. Victim and tormentor are not only social polarities, they are also erotic polarities, both part of a libidinal arrangement. That is why, in all that perversion, there is something like love which, in the end, passes through. Relationships of domination and servitude

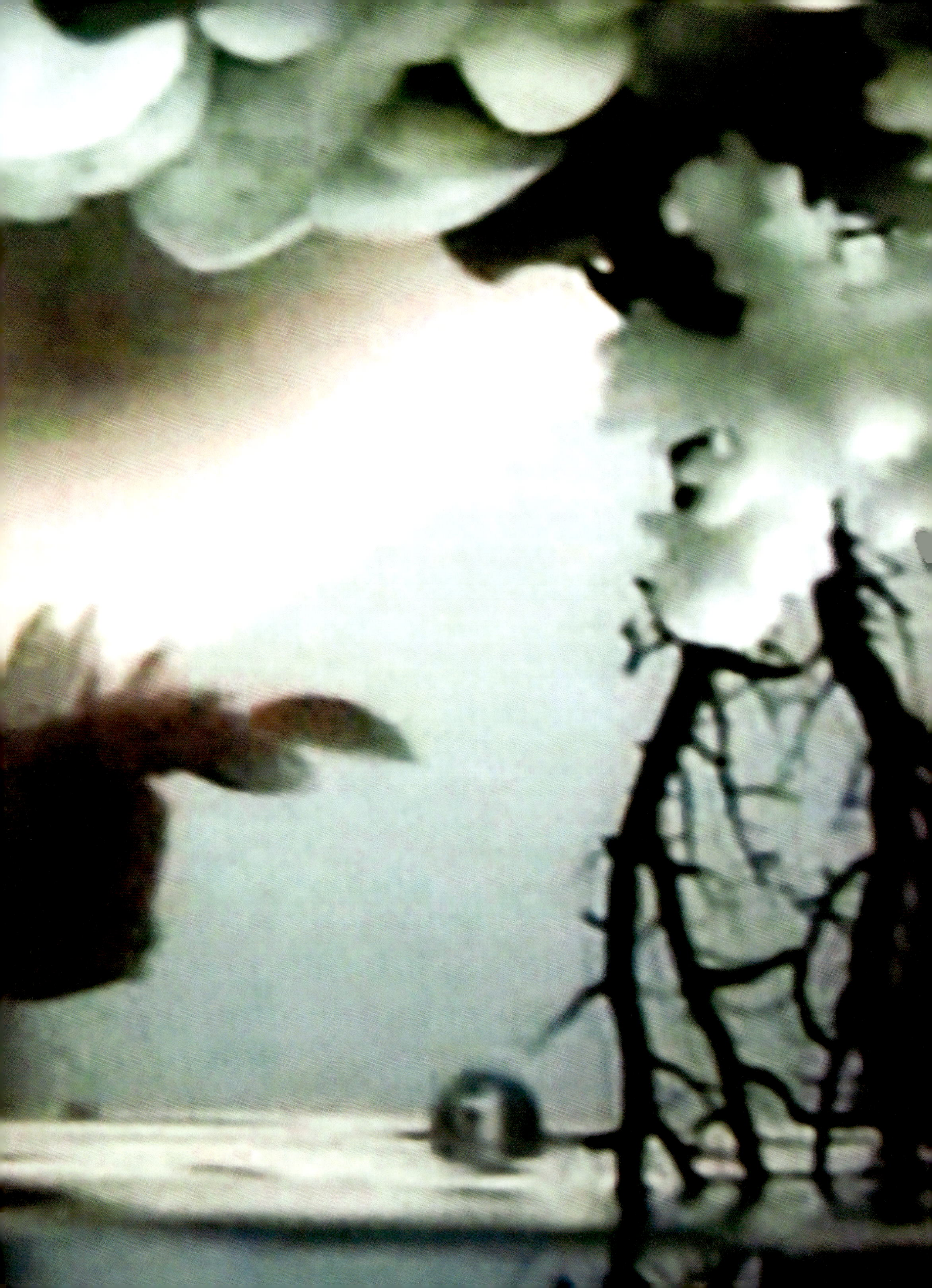

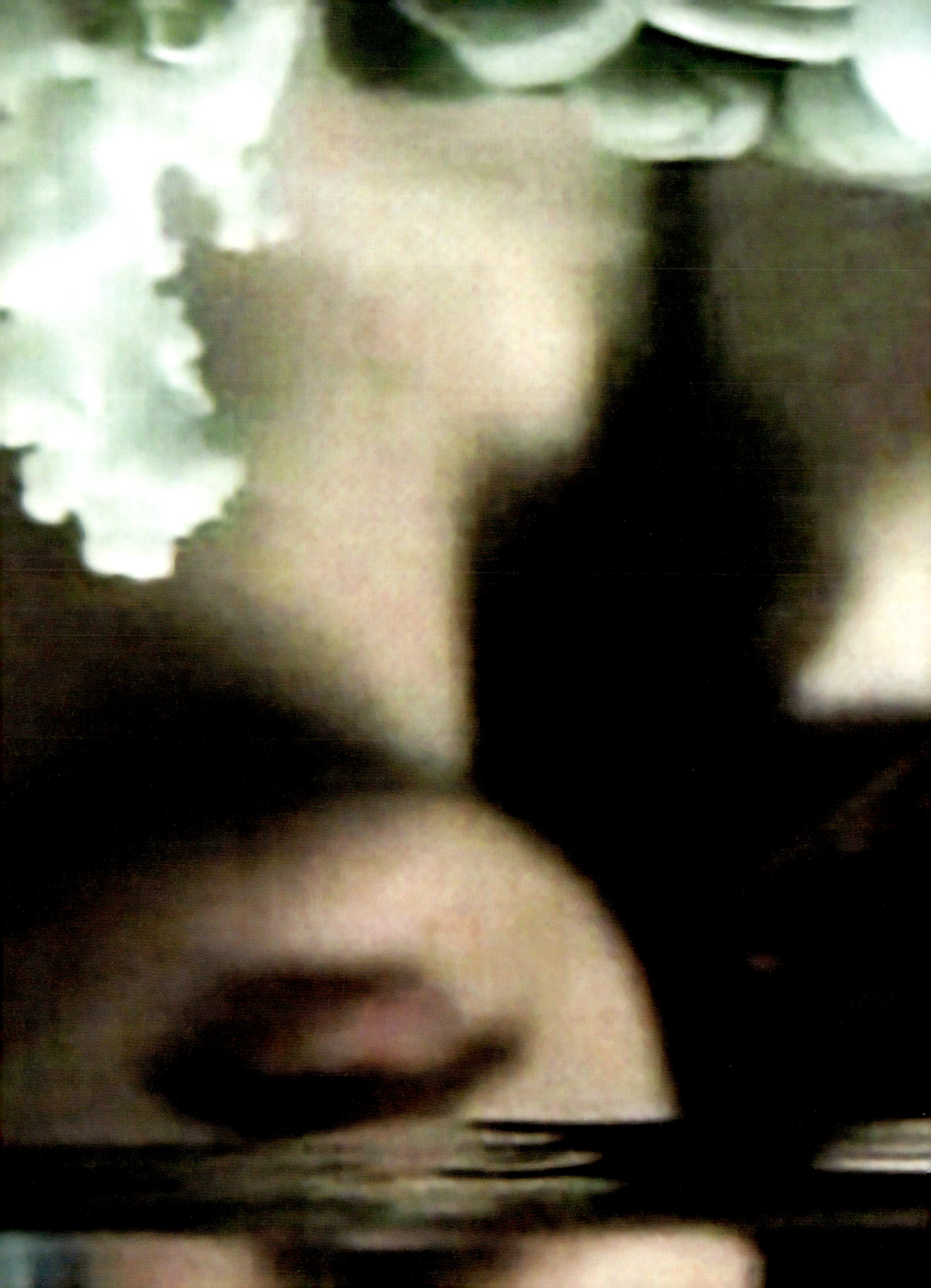

obviously cross the social body and women are most of the time men's property (the character played by Denis Lavant in *Wild Animals* is forced to *buy* Corinne from the man who is not even her pimp), but desire invades those relationships in the shape of a complex sado-masochism. No love without perversion; that such a discourse, even in the Western world, could still, two centuries after Sade, be taken for cynicism, let us guess the intensity of teeth grinding it must cause in Korea. Feminists who had been shocked by the image of women perhaps made a mistake on the nature of representation: Kim Ki-duk doesn't care for being edifying. He doesn't claim a kind of naturalism either: he rather gives the impression of wanting to buy back what could be, but without illusion, starting from reality in its most violent figures, without playing with the tragic. Those fluxes of violence have "to be catharticized". The prostitute plays a part in the equilibrium of the social body, neutralizing those fluxes which go through her, transforming them into money, thanks to which the event itself, the 'quickie', as an emotional debt is cancelled: the prostitute has sex, but nothing happens, it is not an event, it is not the start of a love story; it does suspend thus the irreversibility of what is happening. On that matter one finds remarkable pages by Jean-Francois Lyotard: "the prostitute transforms the client's *jouissance* into money and thus converts, phlegmatically, the perverse libido, or simply its use, the surplus of pulsional energy scattered in society, and dangerous for society, mortiferous because capable of making it go in all directions with no regard for its organic unity" (*Economic Libidinale*). One could thus reverse the relationship: it is not the client who buys back the prostitute, it is the prostitute who buys back the excess of desire of the client (the leftovers of all divisions and social gaps), but that buying back has no moral sense: its meaning is purely economic, like a bank buys back a debt – to invest it in a love relationship.

The genesis of signs

As the suspension of all laws gives birth to an absurd game of endless running into debts and payments of debts, and consequently to a kind of primitive and cruel jurisdiction which one never leaves free nor undamaged, the determined mutism of the characters paves the way for a summary and abrupt communication, a kind of primitive and stuttering language: a staging of pain and cruelty. In the desert of signs, in the defeat of abstractions, it is the body itself which changes into a sign: the young man in *Wild Animals* plunging a knife into his hand to prove his determination, the girl in *The Isle* putting fishhooks in her vagina to force her lover to stay.

Logically, no more than words, things are symbols straight away. They become symbols either in the course of the film, or in the course of the body of work. Kim Ki-duk tries to think cinematographically, with the most stubborn sincerity, the possibility of a relationship between human beings, and to be able to do that he cannot presuppose a system of symbols common to the protagonists and the spectators. He must try hard to show how, on the contrary, things themselves start to make a sign, or how the characters find a way to be connected by something they share. The fishhook in *The Isle* neatly represents that process.

A mute young woman manages a hamlet of floating houses scattered in a lagoon and occasionally sells her body to her tenants. She establishes with one of them, an apparently restrained, calm young man, a special relationship made of silent observation, approaches and flights. Something decisive happens when a police launch tours the huts and the young man so tempered, undertakes to swallow a bunch of fishhooks. For it is not only a violent gesture, it's also a bizarre one. Impossible not to see in that a way, if slightly crazy, unnecessarily bloody, and unnecessarily visual, to kill oneself (with almost ritual aspects, like a kind of little sepuku, if not entirely a suicide, then a bit like a *sacrifice*). The girl hides him, saves his life, and by doing that, gets him into debt. Now something has happened. Perhaps in the past they have slept together, but it was prostitution, that didn't *count*, for every event or debt in the 'quickie' has been neutralized by money. Nothing overlapped the trading. Later when it is the girl's turn to stick fishhooks in her vagina, in a scene every bit as painful to witness, she doesn't want to die at all. She reminds him what she has freed him from. And she forces him to free her in his turn. With that reminder she gives meaning to a gesture which didn't have any, which literally was not a *gesture* but *the action of killing oneself*. Repeated but neutralized, in a way represented, played, that action can now become a gesture, meaning the substance of a sign, as it is a prayer she addressed to him to stay. That repetition of the action, though it does not change the nature of the action, no longer kills, but makes a sign. A prayer infinitely more constraining than a word. Suppose the mute girl is not really mute (like the false mute in *The Bow* who, occasionally, whispers oracles), language would not hold that power. Language demands no sacrifice, one can freely lie without paying the price, without it reaching the liar in his own body, while the girl who communicates that way *cannot lie*, and that is because she certainly couldn't do herself so

56 ▶

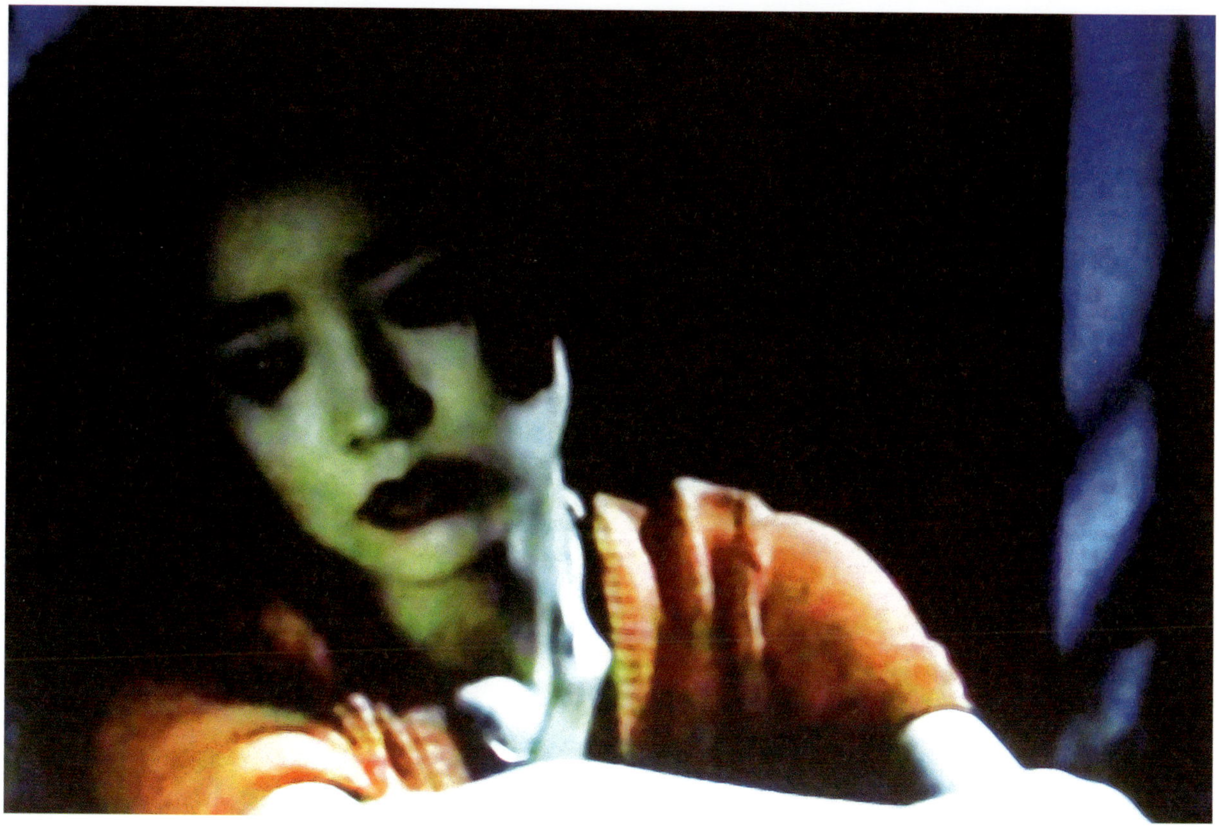

much harm *for nothing* that the young man is so totally forced to come to her rescue. The bringing into play of the body and more precisely the gratuity of violence one forces upon it, produces in reality something like symbolics. A repetition of the violence exerted on one's body, but a neutralization of its suicidal intention: in the emptiness created by the gratuity of what has metamorphosed into a gesture, something passes, something happens, the reminder of a debt and the injunction given to the young man to stay.

It is not by leaving the register of violence that one reaches meaning. It is by emptying that violence of all justification, in the beginning of a ritual, and by diverting violence from its end. The violent action can become gesture and sign. The gesture of the mute girl is the representation of the action to which it is however identical. Identically savage and atrocious, but however, staged. The same thing, but acting its own part. That is the primitive reduplication which makes a sign. The sharing of a wound was necessary, the transformation of a wound in a sign of mutual recognition, in order that relations without deceit happen. The fishhook ends up symbolizing the difficulty of the irretrievable, without the harshness of which there would be no reason to start something like a shared story. What's the use of risking betrayal, lies and murder?

The sacrificial reparation

Still the passage to a system of symbols doesn't mean only the beginning of a story: the ritual repetition can undoubtedly become sign (of a debt), but also acts more generally as the balancing of forces, as the reparation of the insignificance. Every being, when he desires, ravages something, and leaves it there, *in suspense,* which is exactly the definition of anxiety: the unsolved leftovers of unfinished stories, unpunished crimes, and that cancer spreads, mixes in with everything, spoils everything. Thus a sacrifice is needed. It is necessary to take up, to repeat the original action where the anxiety stemmed from. Hence the bizarre gesture of Yeo-jing in *Samaritan Girl*. Prostitution still, but free this time from a relationship to the dominant: a teenage girl, Jae-young, amicably pimped by her girl friend Yeo-jing, sells her body to finance a trip to Europe (unless in this case, the pimp is Europe). But that plan remains unfinished: caught by the vice squad, she choses to throw herself out the window rather than be caught. Yeo-jing, who couldn't stand her friend being a prostitute, is suddenly in possession of a useless hoard of money, suddenly become

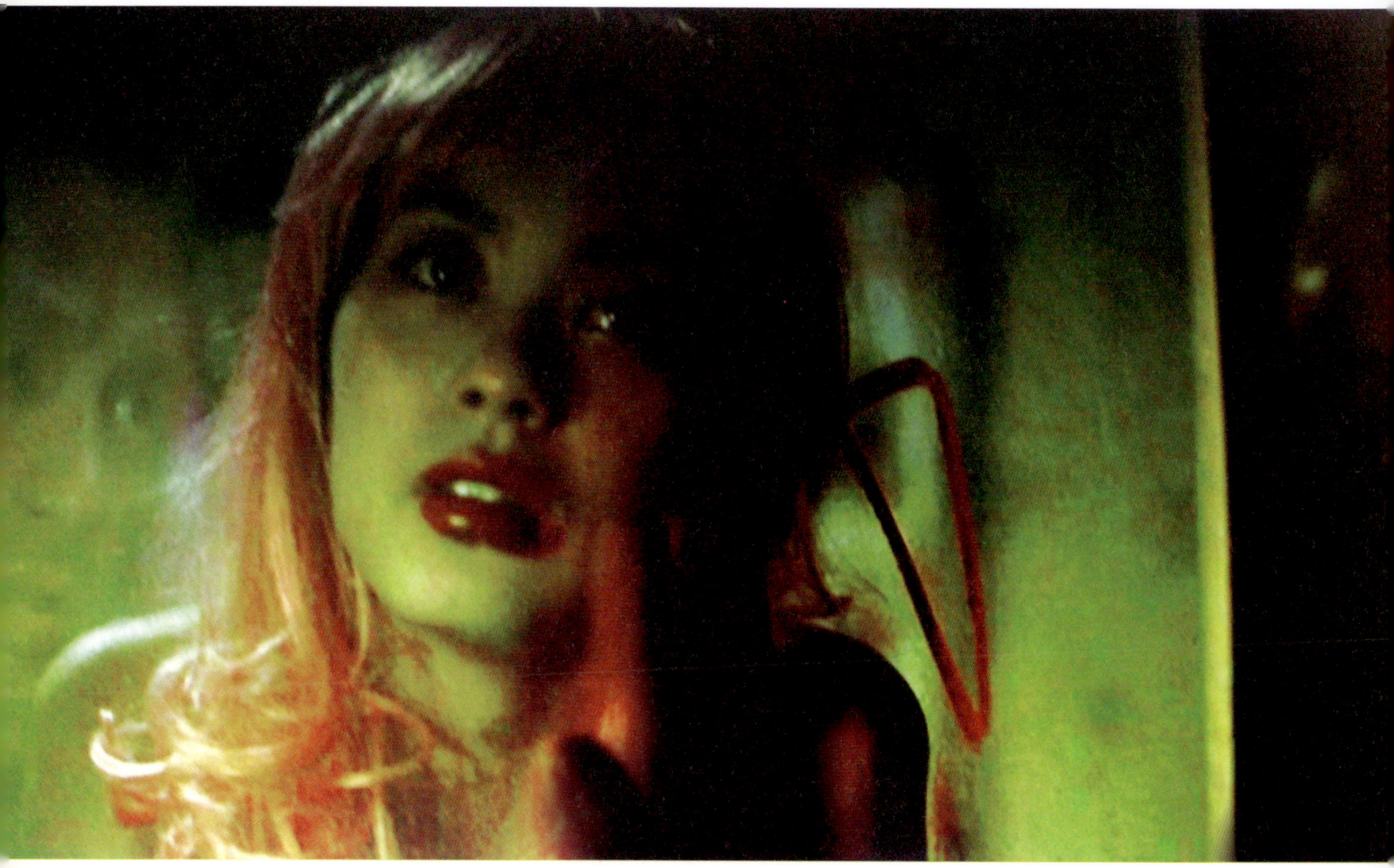

57 ▲

something *surplus*, the incarnation of excess itself. No longer a debt of someone towards someone else, but debt in its pure form, a cosmic surplus preventing harmony. What to do with that thing in suspense? How to suppress it? Giving it back to the clients wouldn't be enough, for it would be nothing more than a gesture, that wouldn't cancel what that money contains, all those 'quickies' whose payment it is, all that weight of pain, life, flesh, whose symbolizing it is. So Yeo-jing, in her turn, will have to pay with her own body in order to get rid of the money, repeating the action in reverse, undoing while doing. If Jae-young was securing a balancing, half-sacrificial, half-accommodating, of social forces, Yeo-jing secures a balancing of cosmic forces. For in reality Yeo-jing doesn't prostitute herself, she doesn't take the money of the men she *gives* herself to, precisely; she repeats, step by step, Jae-young's prostitution, but the action being separated from its conclusion, it becomes a ritual gesture, with which the action is reversed: now the clients are the prostitutes, since it's their turn to receive the money. At the end of the day, they would have paid themselves in an act of prostitution whose order of terms (prostitute-client) will have been abolished.

The repetition of that process leaves nothing to chance, as its use in *Spring, Summer, Fall, Winter... and Spring* bears witness. So, the young disciple, after having tortured a fish, a frog and a snake is forced by his master to go in search of his victims while carrying a stone on his back. Becoming thus the symbolic victim of his own crime, so as to neutralize the relationship between victim-torturer and the inequality left in suspense. Repetition which in *The Isle* was producing signs of communication, here produces sacred signs.

But repetition functions then in the closed universe of the monastery. Unlike the hero in *Spring...* the heroine in *Samaritan Girl* must still confront another violence: her father's misunderstanding. The conduct she has to adopt on one side to secure some harmony contributes, on the other, to producing trouble. Obviously she doesn't try explaining herself: the religiosity, the sanctity of her gesture couldn't survive its enunciation. The difference is absolute, thus tragic: the father can't do anything else than symbolically kill his daughter, the daughter cannot do anything else than to accomplish her silent sacrifice. For there is something more important than the respect due to one's father; in Kim Ki-duk's films, family is part of the old institutions, oppressive and now meaningless, or else simply *impossible*, gnawed from within by rivalry or prostitution (as in *Birdcage Inn*). *Address Unknown* gives a terrifying example: a son cuts his mother's breast to take revenge on her for not having a father, while a little while later, the mother eats her dead son. Family no longer functions, either collapsing from within in a regressive and monstrous autophagy, or tearing itself apart till it dies. In its non-functioning, it carries on, like the law, like the army, to prevent something from happening, and to lead to the morbid all that is trying to make a way between closed worlds.

Vanishing lines

But it all happens as if Kim Ki-duk, in his films, was trying to draw vanishing lines, to escape from the endless running into debts which, at the end of the day, always demand a sacrifice. "As I make films I change my mind, my vision of the world and life changes," he declares. The first films hardly offer any vanishing lines, and, when they happen, they lead to madness or death. As in *Coast Guard*, for example, but also in *Samaritan Girl*, in which Jae-young incarnates, more than any other characters in Kim Ki-duk's films, a kind of immediate innocence. That is precisely what first puts Yeo-jing beside herself: she doesn't understand why her young friend, in the middle of what is supposed to be the worst defilement for a woman, is always *laughing*. A funny vanishing line for, with her laughter, Jae-young defuses all violence: one can have sex with her, but one cannot reach her, one cannot *soil* her. She invents for herself a kind of inviolability. It is as if, with her laughter, she was dodging the flux of violence: one can carry on banging her, sexually obviously, one cannot see the effect on her. Violence can be unleashed: as in Taoism, she has to refrain from echoing it, from holding onto the intensities of pain or humiliation which pass over the body, from appropriating anything. Then violence goes away because there is nothing left to *hurt*, for one has made oneself impregnable. For want of being able to really save one's body from blows and rape, one made disappear what was there to be beaten, to be raped: oneself. How kind becomes that prostitute which isn't one, who, strangely would like to *save* the men she has sex with. Even her death makes her smile: she smiles as she jumps into the void, she still smiles on her death bed, scandalizing Yeo-jing who hasn't still earned the innocence, who will only reach it through inverted prostitution which she will practise later, finding in her turn that silence and that smile which were those of her dead friend.

It is, however, in *3-iron* that the less morbid and purest vanishing line is traced. The film tells the story of a young man, Tae-suk, who enters empty houses, but not to burgle them: on the contrary, he mends what no longer works, lamps, electric goods and domestic bits and pieces. An innocent repairing angel whom no door stops, but who, at a given moment, like all the other characters, must face the law. Once again the conflict is the effect of the irruption of desire, that felt by Tae-suk for Sun-houa, a young married woman he meets, without exchanging a word, in one of those houses. And it is in his jail, once in irons, that he will begin to *become invisible* for good. The jailer, not seeing his prisoner in the reduced angle offered by the spy hole in the cell door, is forced to go in, but, in spite of the smallness of the place, in spite of its wan homogeneous light, cannot see the one who, even in this prison, is only a tenant, an absolute nomad who never blends into the places he *haunts*. As in the darkest forest, the keeper stands quietly in the middle of the cell, like an animal on the lookout for the slightest trace (shadow, movement, breath) where the *material* presence of the prisoner would be betrayed, the prisoner of whom one no longer knows what precisely is imprisoned. The jailer's anger is coupled with total incomprehension: what's the use, he asks, for I shall end up finding you, and since I shall find you, I shall beat you to punish you? What sense is there in that, for you haven't really escaped, for you will not *really* escape my blows? During that time Tae-suk hides behind him, in the shadow of his jailer, like a double, accompanying all the movements of the man who, in those few tiny square metres, is anxiously looking for him. His anxiety alone is enough to prove the success of that escape without escape, that escape *on the spot*. The character dodges the violence by sparing himself, in reality itself, a zone of indiscernability between presence and absence, between matter and spirit, to such a degree that it is the jailer who thinks he's becoming mad. For if there is no real escape, there is still a kind of escape nevertheless. Violence no longer touches him. Once Tae-suk is freed, it doesn't matter if the owners of the houses he carries on penetrating are present or not. That doesn't change anything now. He can no longer be caught. So, meeting up with Sun-houa again, whose husband had him jailed, he can stand behind him while the husband is kissing her. What better, more beautiful way to foil what can never be, namely the reality, the violence of relationship, the conflicts of desire, discord without salvation?

One can compare that becoming-invisible to that, completely missed, of the young man in *The Isle*: he has not found the parade of the other. When the vice squad combs the lagoon, he doesn't try to hide his body. There is, in his behaviour, something terribly radical and in a sense, *literal*: he doesn't try to make himself disappear from the eyes of others, to disappear "metaphorically", but to disappear all together. A becoming-invisible which, on

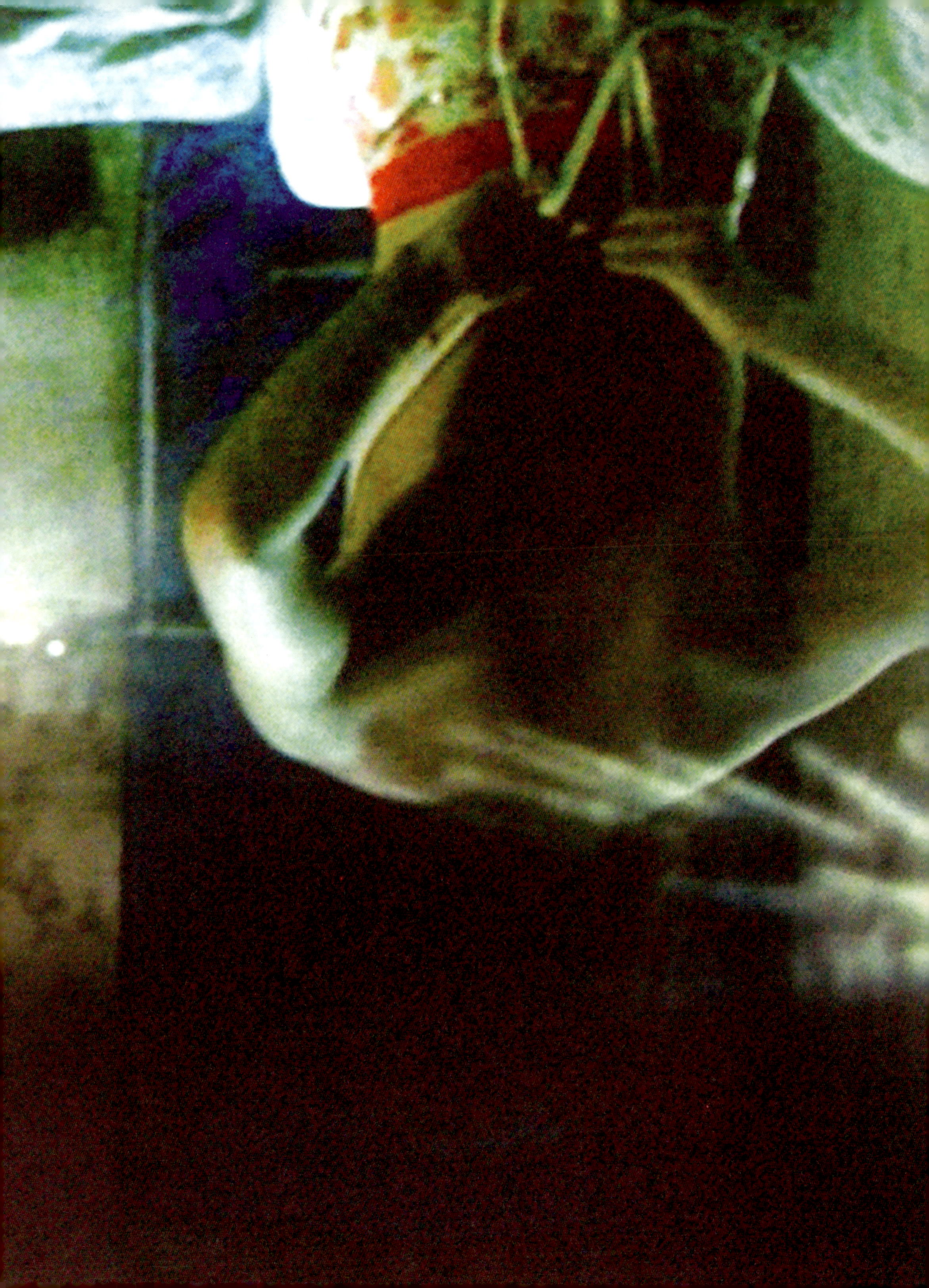

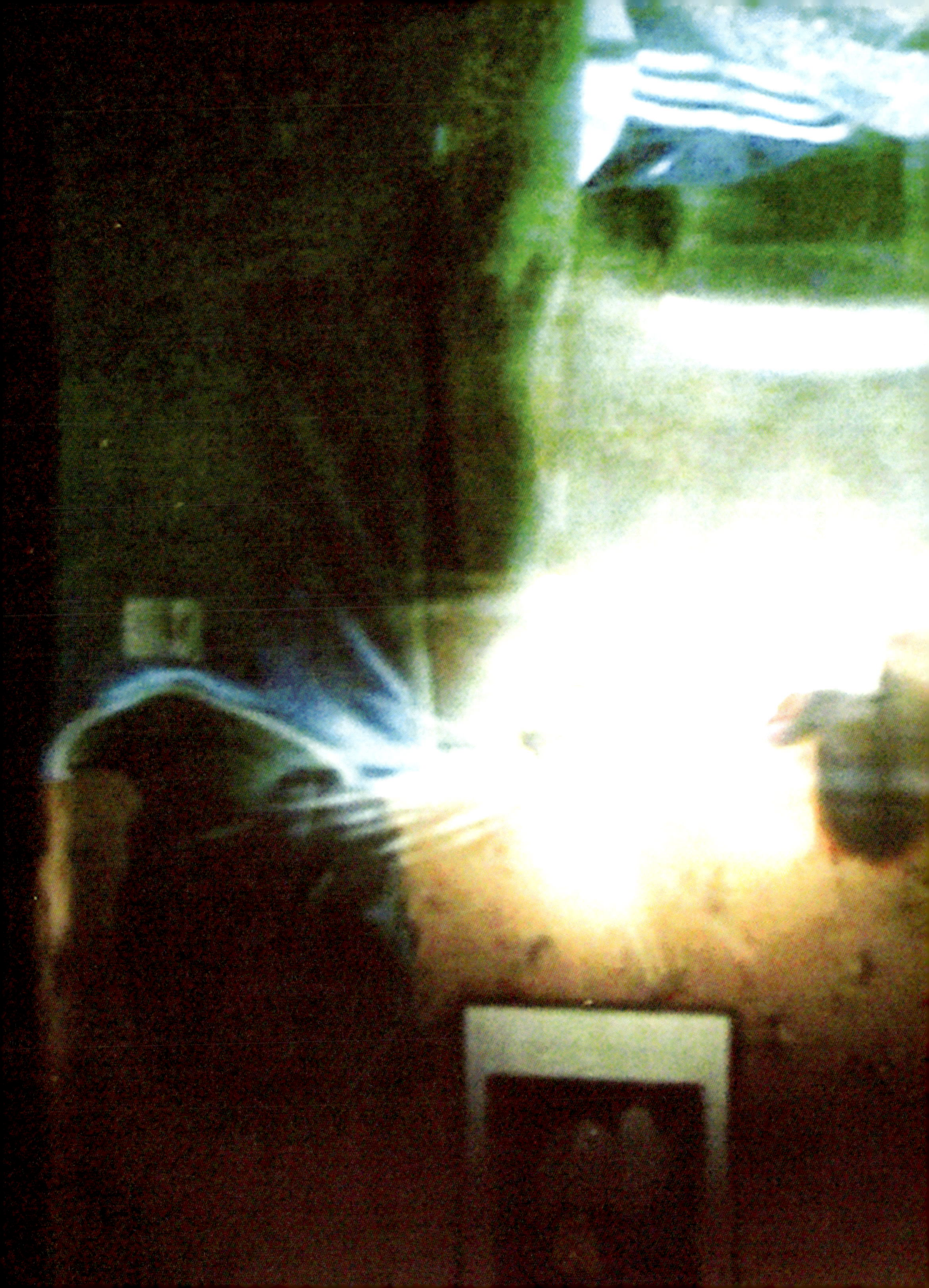

this occasion, could have been paid for with his own death. That is what allows us to think the parade in *3-iron* like the outcome of a persistent search by the director, as if he never really wanted to give up on the possibility of an escape which was not morbid. The progressive sliding into silence in the course of his career bears witness to that too: first, a forced mutism, the irreversible symptom of a sustained violence, it slowly becomes a *chosen* silence and place of purity, as in *Spring...*, as in *The Bow*. A silence which, instead of renouncing forever the possibility of a meaning covering the absurd, which, instead of being consequently the negation of all words, becomes, on the contrary, the supreme possibility. The whole language is thus saved, in a disappearance which is equal to that of the tenant: it exists entirely as silence, thanks to which *poetry* will now be possible. It was necessary for the words to stop going astray, to become once again that silent manufacturer of meaning which saves us from the absurd, so that, for example, making love becomes possible again. For, as Lacan said, "to make love, as its name indicates, is poetry" (*Encore*). One can easily see the evolution from *Bad Guy*: Hang-gi could only love Sheon-Hwa when he was concealed by the artifice of a two-way mirror which physically separated them, a device generally known in Korea only for its by *the police*. "Those windows which divide the people," Kim Ki-duk explains on that subject, "are at the same time easy and difficult to break." Hang-gi's invisibility costs a lot: no less than the physical reality of sexual intercourse. Sexual intercourse is only possible when neutralized, transformed into an inoffensive image on a window, in a way, *cinema*. The tenant's invisibility, on the contrary, costs him nothing. His sexuality is real, concrete, and the huge social cost of that sexuality, whose previous attempts have turned to the morbid, is only paid here through a symbolic disappearance. That was the secret: it was merely a question of becoming nobody. What prevented something from happening was that sedimentation of a closed individual, of a more or less fictive self, or even better, strictly *defensive*, existing only as revolt against the outside violence, around a first humiliation – a bit like when the skin around an infected wound becomes hard and red. But if the person, in their social reality, disappears, if they only remain in the state of a ghostly and repairing presence, meaning: what is left of life when one has taken away everything on which violence could be exerted, only then can the windows be shattered. That is also what *The Bow* shows: it is through the disappearance of his physical reality and, with it, that of old age which forbad him to possess the girl, that the old man can break the window and, as a ghost, in that little bit of surviving life which he is left with, make love to her. That is the unique parade to the absolute difference, the only vanishing line perfectly vanishing: no longer violence, no longer the lie, but invisibility.

To become nobody is an old theme in Buddhism, which *Spring*... echoes: its characters no longer have a name. If one is nobody, one hasn't got the desire to possess, no more that the desire to kill. Thanks to his anonymity, the old monk in *Spring*... slips into the infinitely fragile equilibrium of a big whole.

Surplus becomes the picture

In *Spring*..., specifically, and even more in *The Bow*, another line appears, at work since the beginning perhaps, but concealed, veiled by the roughness of the image, as in *Wild Animals*, Kim Ki-duk's second film, which, despite a rather dull photography, puts us on the right track: at the start we are shown the young anti-hero arriving at the painter's place, beating him till he draws blood and, with that blood, finishing the painting in progress. The flow of blood is not only, in Kim Ki-duk's films, the proof that something is happening. Or should we say rather: if through blood, something happens, it is by virtue of its *visual* reality. Through its outpouring, something *makes it a picture*. The privilege of blood from the point of view of its symbolic power is not only due to the fact that it gives a price to the gesture which accompanies it, but also to the fact that it is violently visual. Cinematographically, it causes a stir. An aesthetic imperative is found where one didn't expect it, where the characters are absorbed by their survival only, an imperious image-making where the sense of Kim Ki-duk's artistic gesture can be read implicitly: the image aspires to a visual reparation of violence. The ritualization of the original violence, by diverting it from its blind insignificance, transforms it into a painting, a flag, a banner, a visual and aesthetic sign *displayed* there. The outpouring of blood transfers all the violence into the visual character of blood. Let us think only of the incredible scene of abortion in *Coast Guard*: the mad young girl immerses herself in the fish tank, whose form itself, a parallelepipedal, calls to mind the frame of a painting, or a television, and whose transparency is slowly clouded by the purple opacity of her blood. The event is not softened, nor its violence diminished by the colour. On the contrary, the colour magnifies the intensity, but, doing so, gathers it and limits it. Through the device of the fish tank, the blood doesn't flow anywhere nor in vain: the fish tank, on the contrary, receives it, keeps it, and transforms it into a painting. The intensity of the violence is at the same time magnified and redeemed by the intensity of the colour. As if, just as light, in order to be seen, must meet an obstacle, violence, to be bearable, must become an image. Another scene, that of the suicide in *Birdcage Inn*: it's only because of the beautiful red stain on the wrist of the prostitute that the spectator, as

59 ▶

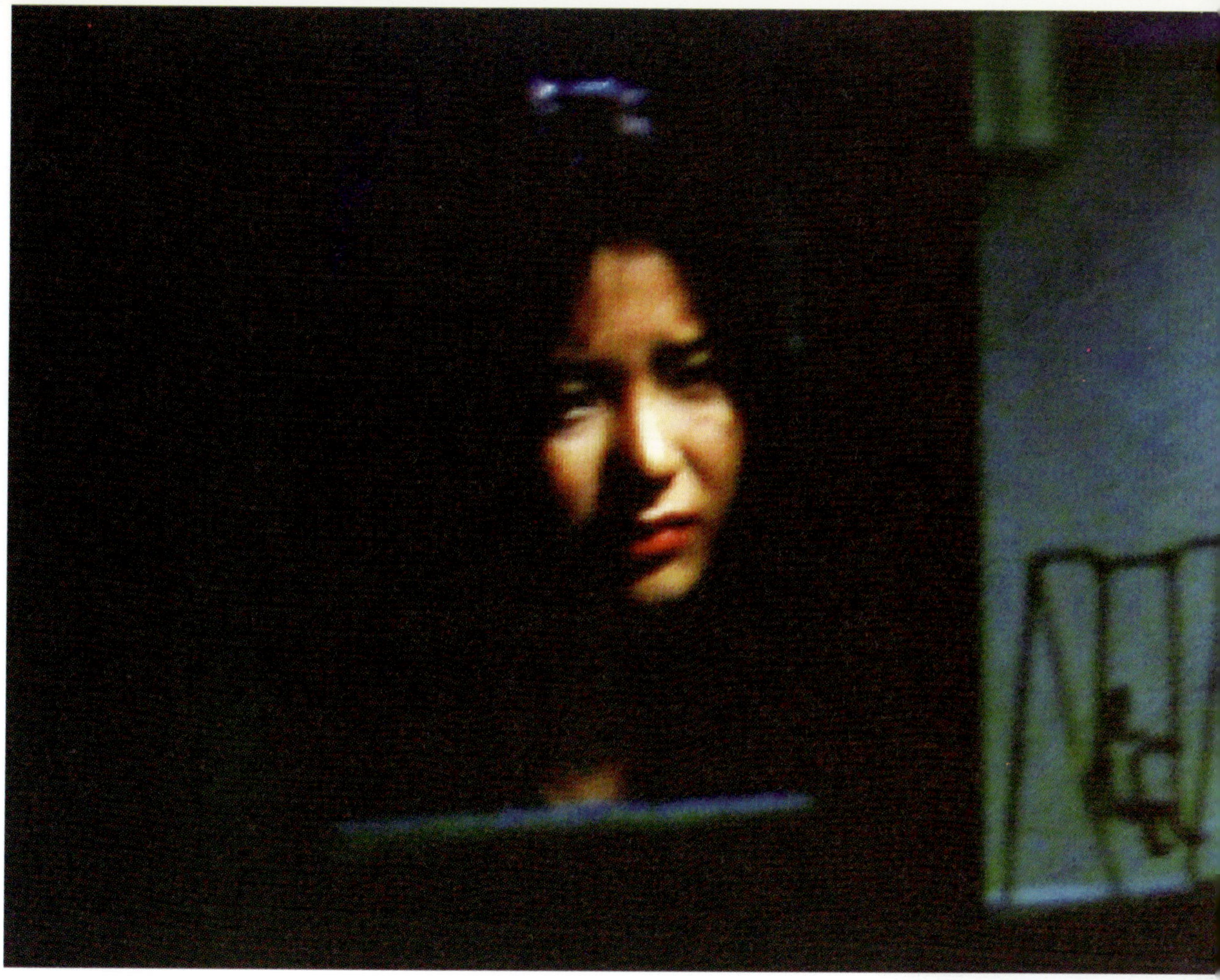

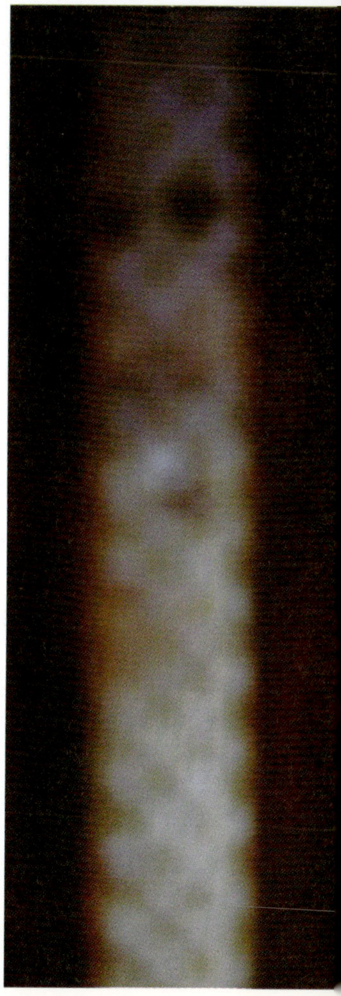

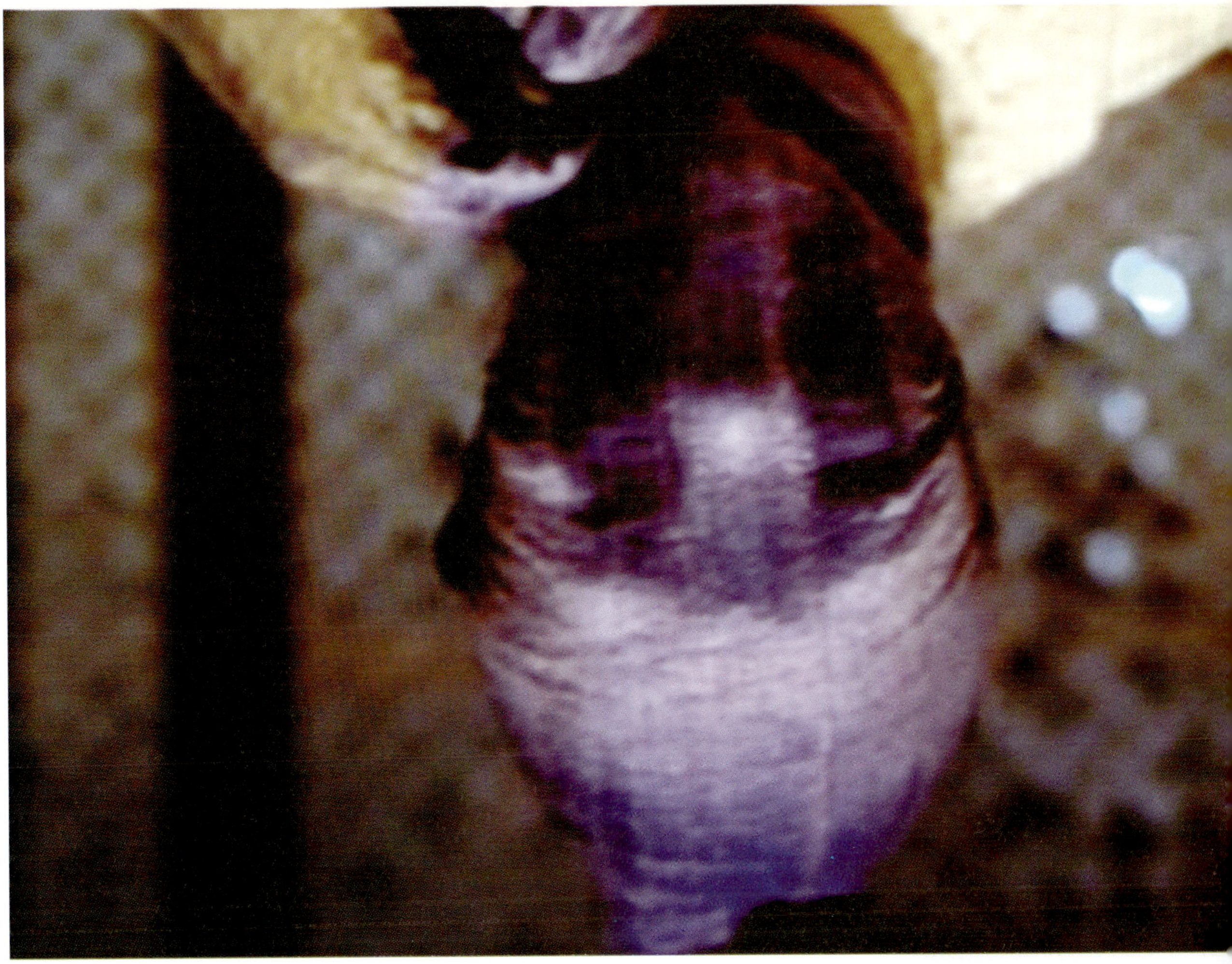

09 ▲

well as the rival, understands that she wanted to die. From the veins of that body, which, from the viewpoint of society is irreversibly spoilt, suddenly appears something pure and bright. The unrecognized Luc Dietrich, being knifed, wrote these extraordinary lines: "Blood flows in the hollow of my hip, my hands can no longer hold it. It is beautiful, it is precious, and it's flowing away. And I marvel that from me, who has eaten so much slime, chewed so much grey food, comes such a red substance." (*L'Apprentissage de la ville*)

That fine line which goes from film to film, slowly reaches efflorescence. So, in *The Bow*, that supernatural and slightly lyrical ending: the old man, having realized that reality contradicted irrevocably the realization of his desire, throws himself into the water. Before that, he fires an arrow into the sky, apparently at random, that one sees later, when the young girl, asleep on the deck, seems to make love to in a dream, planted between her legs. The arrow is the old man's relics, union between the dead and the living, since shot ante-mortem it falls down post-mortem, like the still twinkling light of stars already dead. But, where the arrow fell, blood appears, the blood of lost virginity, *as if* it was the arrow which had pierced her, but also, delicious complication, *as if* the old man had really penetrated her. The arrow produces those two *as ifs* without settling between them, so that the blood remains unexplained, in excess or in suspense, being neither that of the arrow nor that of lost virginity. And it is that excess which, through its sole visual reality and, in a way, by making a painting, testifies to the reality of the event and the irreversibility of the love making. It magically certifies that all is not only a dream. In *Bad Guy*, on the contrary, when Sheon-Hwa, reduced to slavery, loses her virginity, Kim Ki-duk doesn't show the blood: violence is not redeemed by the symbol, it doesn't reach representation in a pictorial form which would limit its effect. The violence here precisely consists in the impossibility to transform that act in a significant event, historical in a woman's life, which underlines *a contrario*, the role of colour (pictorial or musical) in the unforgiving time of decoded relationships: before the artistic display whose example is offered by *The Bow*, the irreparable is not spiritualized, it is an open wound without compensation, without image. With the image, on the contrary, it becomes possible to contain the big haemorrhage of passing time. So the arrow in *The Bow* is not a symbol, but *the* symbol *par excellence*: the presence of an absence. The visibility of the invisible. The image of an image-less, by which the image-less is redeemed. It was already there in the love-making in *Birdcage Inn*, whose beauty seems to redeem prostitution: let's mention the sumptuous shot where the young heroine, in a low-angle shot, makes love on a diving board, or else that other shot, in the bedroom, where the movements of the bodies make the pictorial drapes shake, as if the impossibility of the sexual relationship were, through that, balanced. To gather the excess – the violence – which sets desires against one another, and to make it shine by itself. It no longer is a question of signifying something for one another, but of producing pure signs, artistic signs: in *Birdcage Inn* again, the reconciliation of the "two hostile sisters" happens on a graphic or pictorial mode, only through the fortuitous resemblance of a close-up with Egon Schiele's *The Two Sisters* that one has seen earlier. And strangely, it is from that purely aesthetic reconciliation that the real reconciliation can be felt.

The image is not the only one at stake. It is art in its entirety which transfigures violence. The ultimate metamorphosis of the fishhook in *The Bow* bears witness to that. One can see it too, in a bunch, going into a mouth, that of the girl entrusted to the old man (and those who've seen *The Isle* can't avoid anticipating the damage), but merely in order to stretch a small thread which, held at its other extremity by two fingers, becomes a little musical bow. The fishhook's nature doesn't change, it remains a violent hook, but specifically without that violence it wouldn't catch and the girl wouldn't be able to stretch the string nor to produce sounds. All of Kim Ki-duk's cinema seems from that point of view a metaphorization of the artistic gesture itself. A salvation without recovery, without reparation, without denegation. Peace is always temporary and uncertain, a minute equilibrium between exasperated beings. "Art feeds on that permanent tension," he said about the divided Korea. "I would rather choose peace, even if art should disappear. But humanity has never known peace, and will probably never know it. That is why one needs cinema". That "permanent tension" is that of the bow: at the same time instrument of violence and instrument of music, inseparably. No beautiful formula will ever be found, for music always becomes quiet and turns to violence again, and violence saves itself, either through music where it becomes invisible, or in the image where it lights up. To find harmony facing the irreducible conflicts of human beings, all right, but a harmony in the *musical* sense, a fragile almost-nothing, like that little air played on a boat in the middle of the immense deep-sea silence. So the most beautiful wisdom is perhaps that of the monk in *Spring...*, who writes on a round piece of wood with water – purity, *par excellence* – one sees drying straight away and who, having reached the bottom of the line, starts again, a production without melancholy, *without surplus*, of sacred signs, a writing disappearing like words, like water, like life, which it permanently redoubles and transfigures.

"I want to live stretched like a bow till I die."

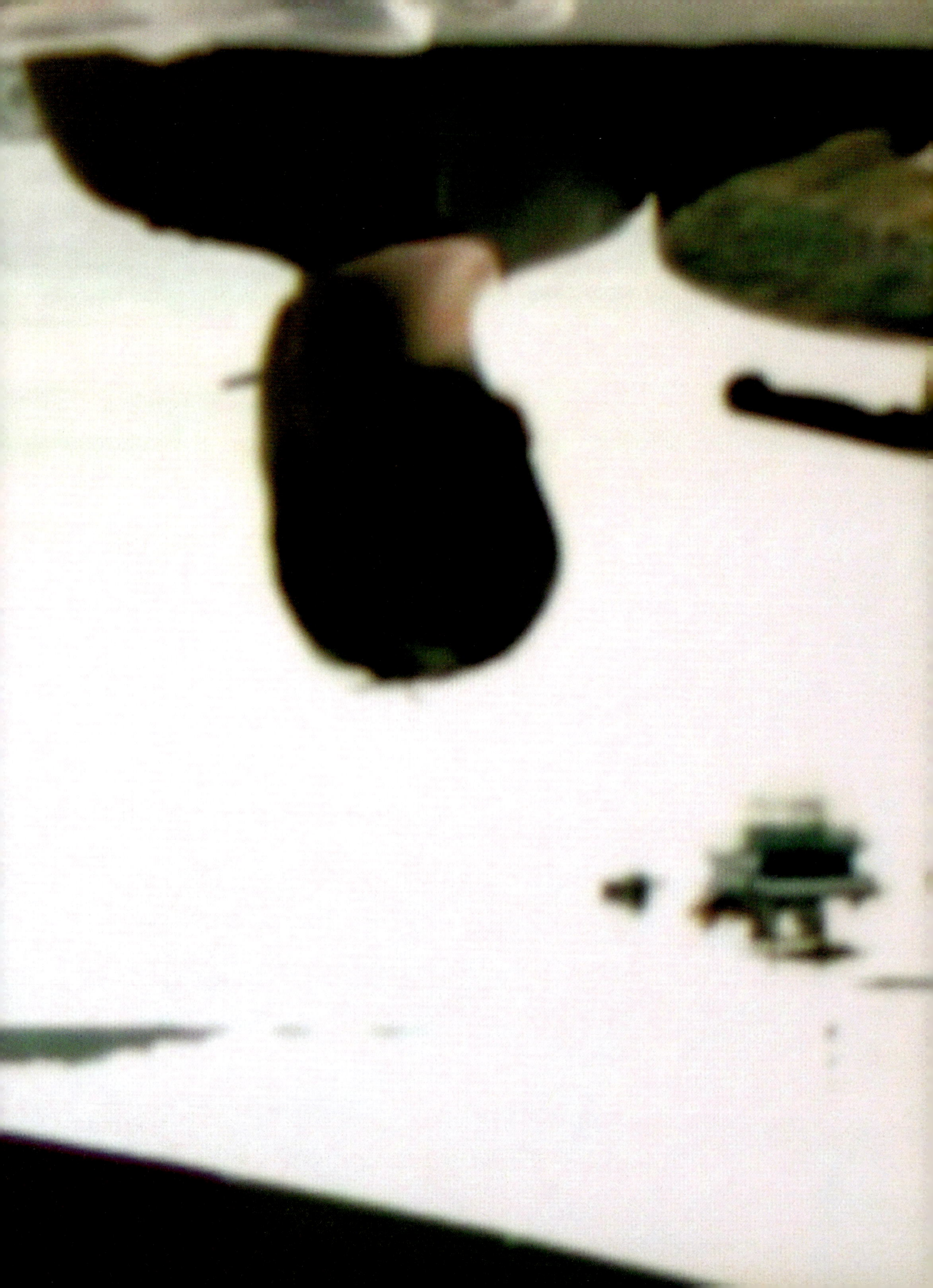

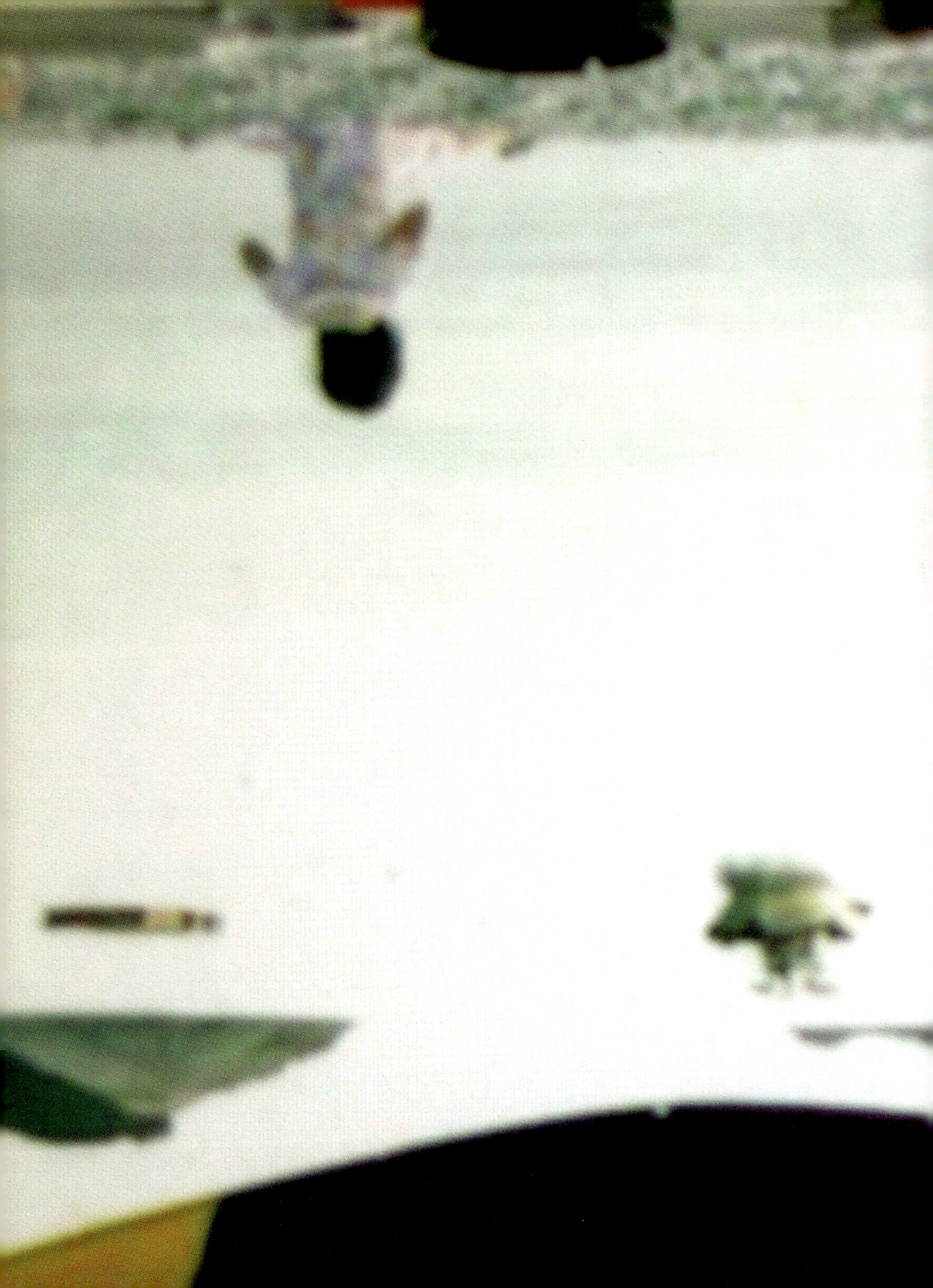

61 ▲ 62 ▼

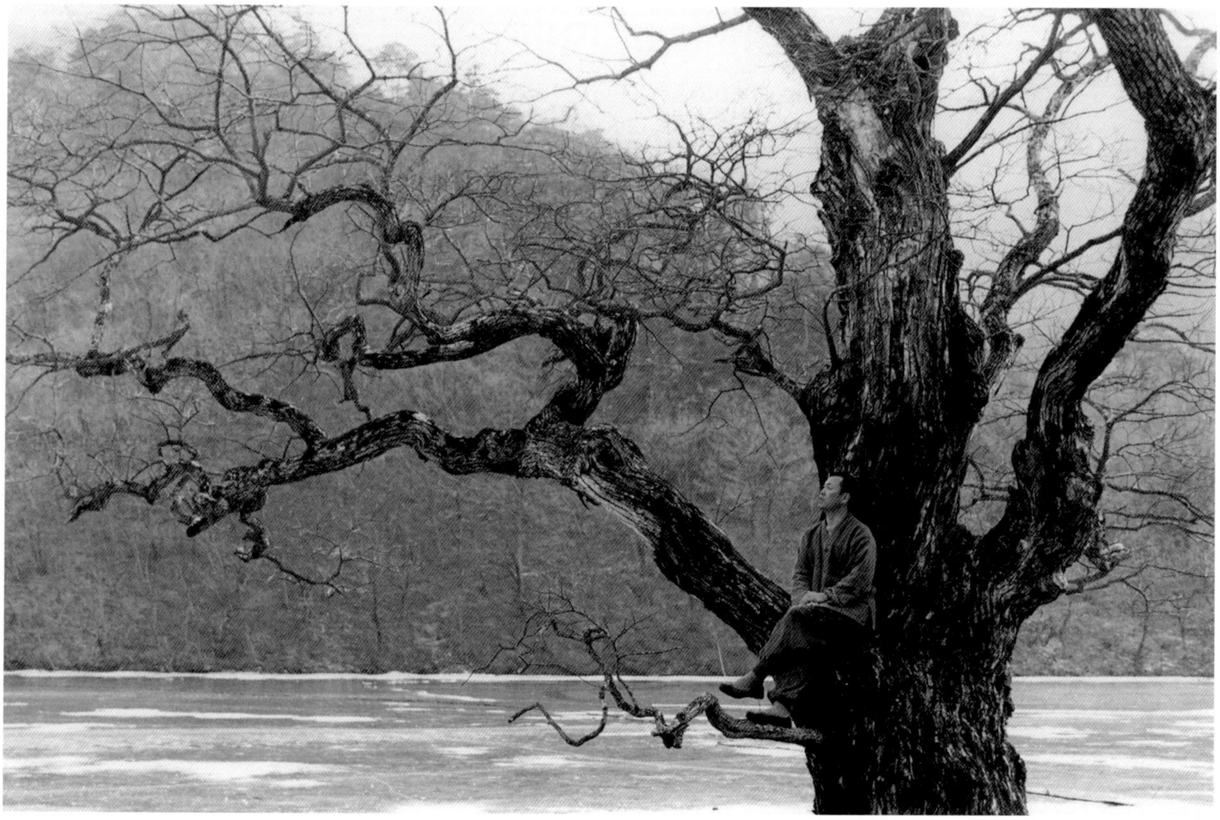

IN THE MIRROR OF SILENCE

The recent breakthrough of Korean films has gradually imposed the cinema of that country as a partner with whom we have to reckon in future. The director Kim Ki-duk has been noticed for the extreme modernity of his films while representing, at the same time, and in a most intimate way, images of a traditional Korea. For me, as an ethnologist and specialist on China, Kim Ki-duk's films paint a portrait of a society that is both familiar and remote. Korea, as China's neighbour, has been its vassal for a long time, and it has thus integrated numerous elements of Chinese culture. The omnipresence of music, in China, as in the work of the director, where it expresses the feelings of the characters, invites us to again question universalism.

For an ethnologist that question is fundamental. Indeed, we go to faraway terrains to try to understand what is "other", what is "different", perhaps also "what we lack". Our postulate is that there is unity in the human world, and that this unity makes possible the study of societies through their differences. What is the use of going as far as Korea, or China, if it is only to reassure us of the idea that our values, supposedly universal and superior, are really the best? Our method consists in studying the social facts while leaning on the differences between the cultures. For if common traits are found everywhere, each society arranges the elements it values in its own unique way.

But what about feelings and their expression? Are feelings truly universal? And does music, which is often their favourite vehicle, have a universal reach?

From music to animals

In most of his films Kim Ki-duk makes little use of spoken words. And when the characters do speak, it is often as background noise, as unimportant conversation. There is never any debate on ideas. The men don't talk, they act. Often set in magnificent landscapes, the men and women face life according to circumstances and their meetings with others. Each time the characters, and particularly the women, are moved, or angry, or terribly sad, it is expressed through music, not words. In reality, Kim Ki-duk's films illustrate perfectly that definition found in an old Chinese classic, the *Book of Music*:

Music is born from sounds. Its source is in the resonance of the human heart produced by its meeting with external beings. Thus, a sad heart produces nervous and abrupt sounds;

a joyful heart produces open and harmonious sounds; a happy heart produces ample sounds; an angry heart produces gross and heavy sounds; a respectful heart produces straight and serious sounds; an amorous heart produces harmonious and sweet sounds. Those six emotions are not internal, but resonate with the action of external beings who bring about transformations.

So emotions are produced by meeting with "external beings". Would it be human beings, or "other" beings: animals, mountains, lakes, islands... women... Each meeting brings its share of surprises... and its share of tearings apart and sadnesses. Are animals, for example, different from men? Kim Ki-duk asks the questions: what relationship do human beings have with those "others"?

In some scenes, cruelty towards animals shocks the Western spectator. Perhaps it also shocks Korean people, even though different societies have views distinct from ours on relationships between people and animals.

One thing which cannot go missing on festive tables in Korea as well as in other Far-Eastern countries are fish, which represent fecundity and abundance. Fish must always be consumed "fresh". The pleasure of sushi is not the prerogative of the Japanese people only; for that reason, fishing is a favourite hobby for Korean people, as is shown several times in Kim Ki-duk's films.

In the Chinese village I'm studying, it is women who prepare the fish. It is first held still on the ground with the left hand. With the right, which holds the enormous kitchen knife, the woman scales the fish, which is, of course, still alive. The fish writhes, opens wide its mouth. I wonder if it feels the same as when the hairdresser cuts our hair, or if it feels pain. Then she cuts opens the belly and takes out the guts. The fish is still alive and floundering. That done, she fillets one side, then the other. At that stage the fish is still not dead, it opens its mouth and continues to make wild movements. The last operation consists in cutting what's left into bits. To the question, "why don't you kill it before preparing it?" women just smile, for that reflection seems so stupid to them. It's always been done like that! What's so strange in that?

The Isle presents the same type of scene when one of the characters who has just caught a fish, cuts out a fillet, then eats with relish his "fresh" sushi with his girlfriend, blood dripping from their lips, while the fish is still floundering at their feet, so much so that the man ends up throwing it back in the water. We then see the fish swimming away in the

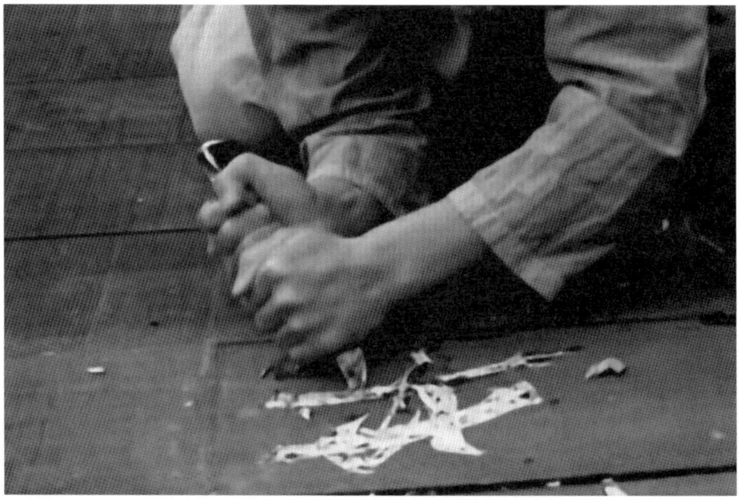

◀ 63

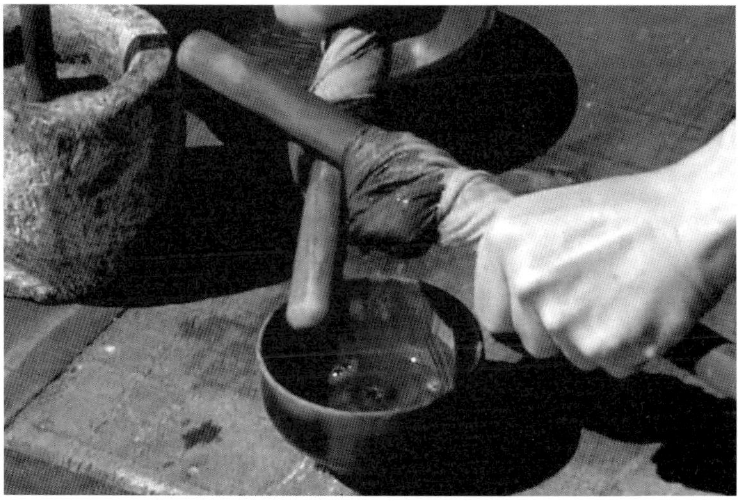

◀ 64

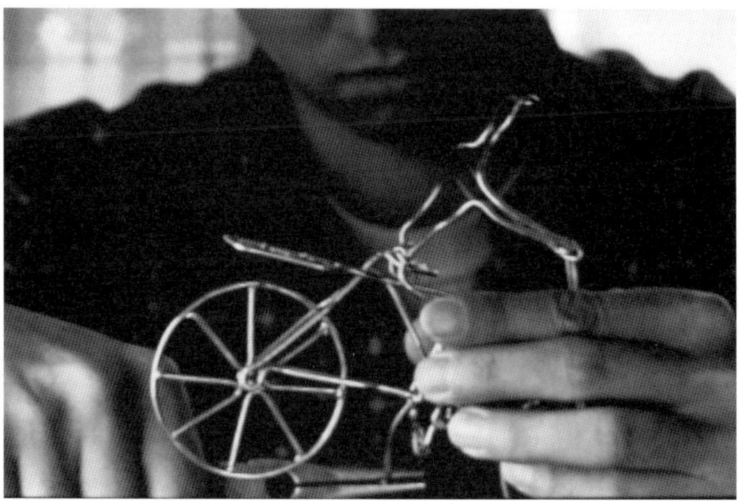

◀ 65

murky water, amputated of one fillet, dripping with blood... One thinks it could also happen to us, to have one arm amputated and carry on living in that state.

In *Address Unknown*, the dogs are beaten to death. Because dog's meat is a favourite dish in Korea, it's also part of the banquet. In Korea too, the dog is "man's best friend", but its meat is nevertheless consumed, without Koreans seeing any contradiction in that. One of the film's characters however feels uneasy about it and is reluctant to beat dogs to death. Perhaps it has something to do with him being of mixed race, for his father was an American soldier who went back to America, leaving a false address, so that the letters addressed to him always come back with the endorsement "address unknown".

Do Chinese and Korean people have no feelings for animals? One learns in the course of the film that it is not so much the butcher's personal cruelty which is at work here, as the absence of any other means to kill the dogs. When one of the characters offers him a gun, he uses it straight away, but his hands are again tainted with blood and he wonders if that killing is in reality any different.

Why does the little boy in *Spring, Summer, Fall, Winter... and Spring* make animals suffer? With his master only for company, on that floating monastery in a lake isolated in the mountains, life is not easy. He only has animals for companions, and no friend, no mother, no father. He is alone with the master, who is benevolent, but hard. The goddess too is severe, and doesn't protect her novice from his inner inclinations.

From animals to women

Among all the animals that appear in Kim Ki-duk's films, fish are present everywhere: in the water of the lake, of course, and in the basin which gathers the rain water; it is also, for those who can recognize it, the "wooden fish", the buddhist percussive instrument that accompanies all prayers. And fish fly in the wind, hung at the four corners of the monastery, under the bells suspended from the overhanging roofing. The paradox is that on the one hand, fish are badly treated, and on the other, they are the object of attention and love: a musical instrument which produces divine sounds; flying in the wind to bring the movements of clouds to the sky; goldfish in a bowl; fresh and delicious flesh. They are always magnificent because of their beauty and their weakness.

In reality, what's the difference between the fish, martyrs in *The Isle*, or the animals tortured in *Spring, Summer, Fall, Winter... and Spring*, and women? All are weak, defenceless, incapable of rebelling against horror. All are dominated. All have suffered or suffer cruelties, which the spectator doesn't always hold the keys to: the girl in *Address Unknown* or *The Bow*, the young woman in *Coast Guard*, the woman in *The Isle*, the Hungarian woman beaten up in *Wild Animals*, the young woman in *3-iron*, the prostitute in *Bad Guy*. Next to those women there is often a man, also wounded, but who rebels, without however having always succeeded in freeing himself. That character is, or becomes, an oppressor, like the pimp in *Bad Guy*, or the soldier in *Coast Guard*. In reality, cruelty towards animals is precisely the same as that inflicted on human beings. Thus it is not that Korean people are less sensitive to animals than Westerners, it is rather that for Korean people, animals and human beings belong to the same order of living beings, and consequently receive identical treatment. The only meaningful differences lie in the fact that human beings suffer, on top of physical cruelties, psychological tortures, and that they possess – to some extent – the possibility for revolt.

Beings all belong to the same order of the living. But the destiny of the weak is to be oppressed. Women who, *par excellence*, represent "the other" for the man, often appear to be oppressed in Kim Ki-duk's films. Is it for that reason that female characters affect the spectator much more than male characters? In contrast to male violence, female weakness is always linked to beauty, physical as well as spiritual, and it invites compassion.

The Western spectator wonders why those women don't try to find ways to leave their hell. But escape is futile, for when they try to leave, they are always recaptured, as in *Bad Guy* or *3-iron*. Moreover, by living with and thus accepting the violence of their male partner, those women slowly transform the misfortune, minimizing it or making it "a little less" horrible. For example, the physically abused woman in *3-iron* doesn't see why she should leave her husband, especially when he beats her less, and when her lover is present at her side. In their way, Kim Ki-duk's female characters are representations of the compassionate Buddha, who appears in *Spring, Summer, Fall, Winter… and Spring*.

From women to male violence

Beyond the stories told in each film, the spectator doesn't know the origin of the calamity or the cruelty. For Kim Ki-duk, it seems that man's nature is caught in the turmoil. However, society is not very present. Obviously, *Coast Guard* denounces military absurdity,

66 ▼ 67 ▼

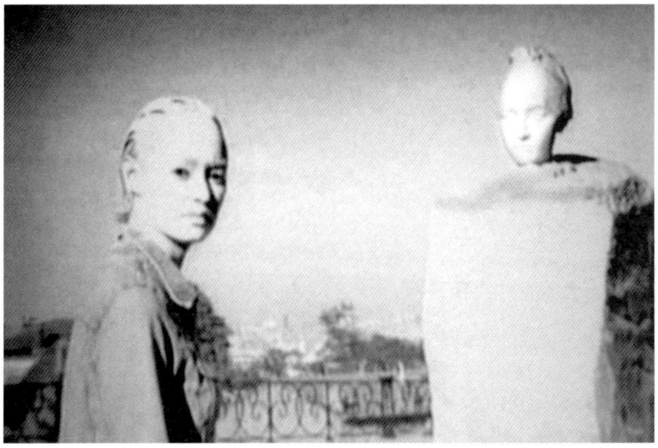

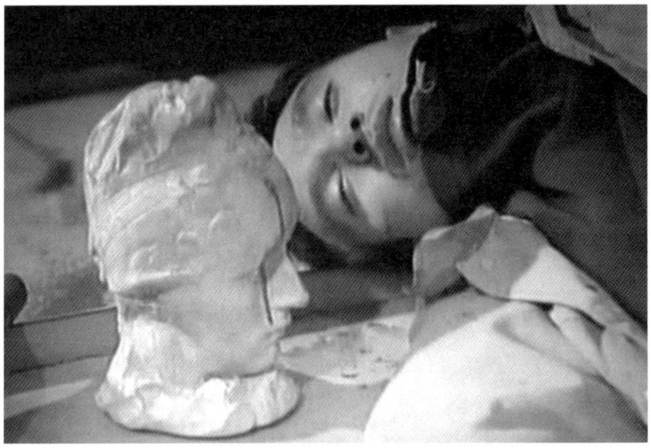

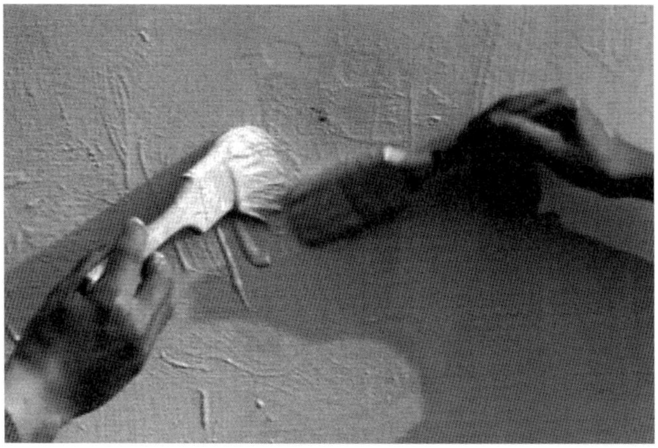

◀ 68

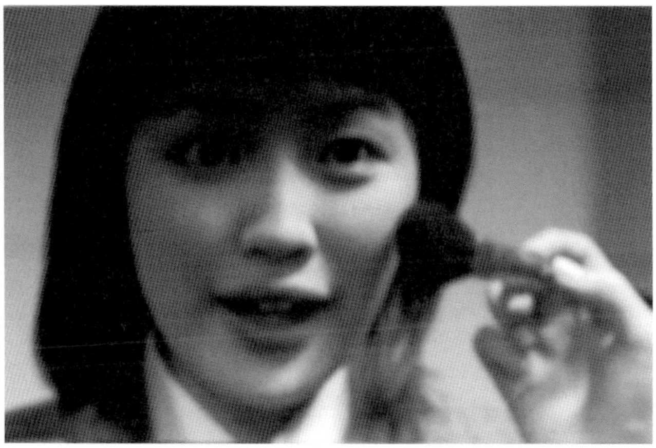

◀ 69

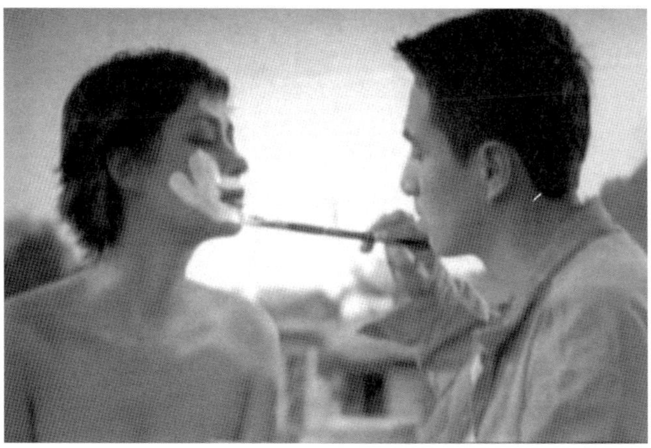

◀ 70

71 ▼

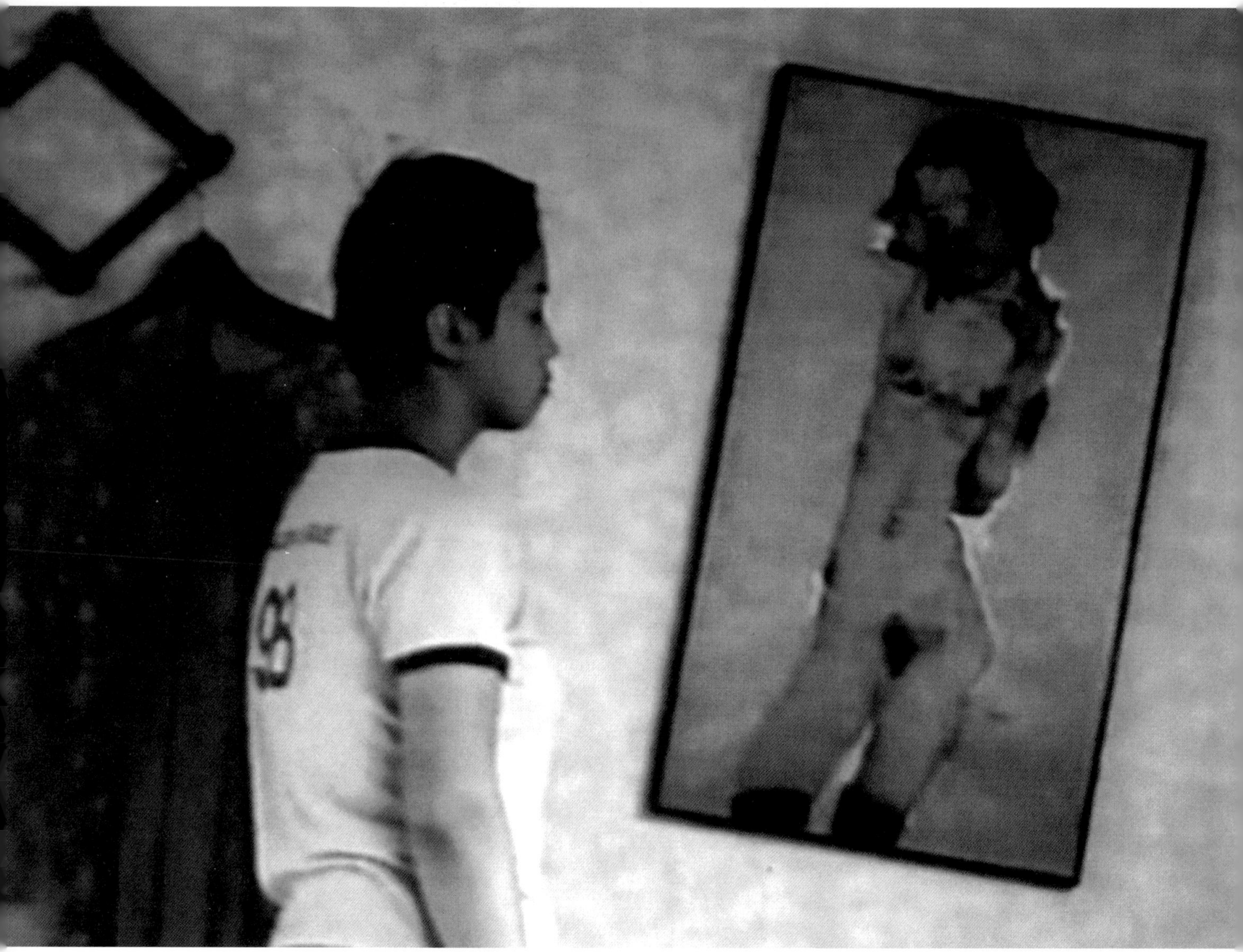

Address Unknown that of the presence of the American army on South Korean soil, *Bad Guy* questions prostitution, *Spring, Summer, Fall, Winter... and Spring*, solitude and religion, etc. Thus, each time, it is a personal point of view that the director proposes, and not a collective representation. If women fall into prostitution, it's because they are weak. If the little boy torments animals, it's because he is so lonely that he is not even aware of his cruelty. If the soldier becomes mad, it is because he is caught up in his obsessions. But beyond the personal circumstances of each of the characters, where does that incapacity to react come from, that insurmountable weakness, recurrent from film to film? The spectator is reduced to suppositions, for the great artist Kim Ki-duk doesn't impose his own answers. By seeing all of his films, which stage paradoxical and contradictory situations, the most perfected probably being the love that the prostitute has for her pimp in *Bad Guy*, one ends up wondering if, somewhere, that weakness doesn't reveal an essential drama, never named, or else just lightly touched upon: that missing North Korea?

As soon as one accepts that interpretation, one realizes that the missing we're talking about is typically Korean. However, the characters' feelings speak to the Western spectator, cross the barrier of culture by telling us essential things which resonate perhaps with the deep structures of our humanity.

Hence, the remarkable use of music in Kim Ki-duk's films. In *3-iron* few words are spoken until the final "I love you". But one doesn't get bored, and the music is enough to make the spectator understand the characters' feelings. It is a "modern" music, thus accessible to spectators. It is not traditional Korean opera, which would grate on our Western ears. And if there is a traditional Korean music, as, for example, the two-string fiddle supposed to be played with the bow in the film with the same name, then it is arranged in a way that makes it seem both strange and exotic, both close and audible. Perhaps universality also comes from that, those beautiful sonorities, though ever so slightly Korean. What is Korean, or what is particular to Kim Ki-duk, is that use of music and the abolition of spoken words, as if those words were only bearers of lies. Only music is true since it always expresses the truth of the characters' feelings, as related in the extract of the *Book of Music* quoted above. That truth is undoubtedly universal, but the way it is expressed in Kim Ki-duk's films is specifically Korean.

The bow presents us with an extraordinary music for it is accomplished with a weapon, thus producing harmony and violence at the same time. In ancient Far Eastern civilisation, archery was part of young men's complete training. In reality, that practise necessitates qualities of self-distanciation and inner calm while being intensely focused on the target. That practise is still carried out today in Korea, as it appears in *Address Unknown* and *The Bow*. In the latter, the bow is also the instrument of divination. South Korea is today one of the countries considered as developed, but it's shamanic past is still very much present. Korean people still seek the advice of shaman diviners to guide them on the path of life. Each time the old man shoots at the girl – the aim being to miss her and not to touch her – the tension is immense: it's a god who is manifested. The violence of shooting brings forward divine words and the music produced by the bow transforms the violence into gentleness. Beware, however: the bow remains a weapon. The girl uses it to shoot at her aggressors. The old man uses it to deflower the girl.

The power of the individual

The treatment of music and the absence of spoken words are equally in keeping with the simple and spare framework of perfection always sought by Kim Ki-duk. It's in keeping too with the system of the Far-Eastern way of thinking relative to martial arts that Kim Ki-duk explores several times in his films. The perfection of the bodily gesture brings power, that's the reason why the man who rebels, or the man who wants a way out, must first of all be in control of himself. That is how the young man in *3-iron,* in the naked cell of his prison, practices assiduously a kind of Kung-fu thanks to which he succeeds in making himself invisible. He slowly controls himself, before controlling his warden. But the lesson is harsh, and he starts by losing. But with each fight, he learns something. Paradoxically, it is the cruel warden who is his master: in the second fight, the young man is betrayed by his shadow, which allows the warden to discover him, though he is hiding behind him. Finally out of prison, the young man begins successfully to put the lesson into practise and settles with the woman he loves, under the nose of the cuckolded husband: he has become invisible for the husband, but remains visible for the woman who can then tell him: "I love you".

Controlling others starts by the perfect control of oneself. There is in that, in an underlying way, an extraordinary faith in human power. In the Far-Eastern way of thinking, man is capable of reaching and achieving a strength that Western people don't even suspect. The young Korean man becomes aware of the extreme power of his being, thanks to the control of his body and his mind. Similar to the Japanese Samourai or the Chinese

Kung-fu adherent, he trusts himself. However, not used deliberately, the power obtained by total self-control, would it be in martial art, golf practise or archery, doesn't bring what has been sought: the old man in *The Bow* will only possess the girl in a symbolic way, through the arrow he shoots and which falls between her legs. In *3-iron* the young man and the betrayed husband will fight without resolving the question of possession of the woman. It is only when the young man has control over his impulses that he will win his battle against the violent spouse. Kim Ki-duk's films paint that Far-Eastern individualism which is to be found not in the conception of the individual as autonomous and independent, but in that faith in the power of the human being, capable of controlling the world.

Though Kim Ki-duk's early films are dark, they become increasingly more optimistic. Will the new little boy in *Spring, Summer, Fall, Winter… and Spring* who tortures a tortoise have the same destiny as his master? That is not sure, for perhaps this time, the goddess, now placed at the very top of the mountain, will be more vigilant. In *The Bow* the girl escapes and leaves with her boyfriend, and the abused woman in *3-iron* keeps her lover at her side.

Kim Ki-duk talks to us about the weakness and the power of human feelings, whether those of men or women. But why have human beings so much difficulty expressing their feelings? Beyond the personalities of the characters, it concerns Far-Eastern civilization, where the human being is primarily perceived as a collective being, meaning in which individual feelings must not interfere with status and social role. That is the reason why music only is able to say what the characters cannot articulate or verbalize. That remarkable use of music is thus, for Kim Ki-duk, a way to denunciate the intransigences imposed by the Far-Eastern conceptual way of thinking to the people who wish to express their feelings.

Because the situations presented are extreme, in a positive or negative sense, they distress and upset us. They make us reflect on life and give us the means of reflection to treat our own ills. That is what a Korean director, for he is Korean, offers us as a present. In reality, the question of universalism is a false problem: rather than a transparence or an equality of men amongst themselves, isn't it the richness that that "other" way of looking brings to the Western spectator that is important in the end?

It's necessary to see Kim Ki-duk's films for what he tells us about Korea. What we discover then brings us something new and unknown. That "something" is in keeping with the framework of Chinese civilization ruled by the system of *yin* and *yang*. That symbol, the emblem of the South Korean flag, which also appears on the boat in *The Bow*, is the underlying structure of all his films. That duality is expressed in the contrast between weakness and power, cruelty and kindness, violence and tenderness, the relationship most often binding a man and a woman. That viewpoint shows us that those opposite situations are connected and that they echo each other. That way of thinking which takes into account the oppositions and contradictions inherent to human life is rather different from our exclusive vision.

In that, Kim Ki-duk's films are typically Korean. Beyond the characters and their pain, it is that missing other, meaning the pain of the partition of Korea, which is expressed in his films. Perhaps we can link the optimism of his recent films to the resumption of dialogue between the two Koreas, as minimal as it still is today.

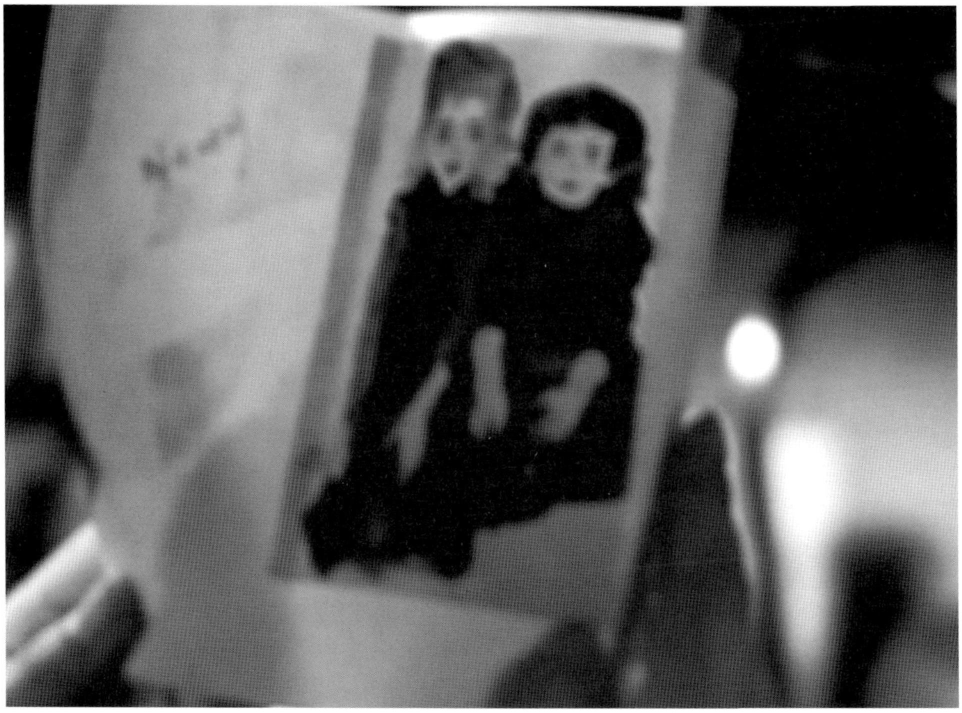
◀ 72

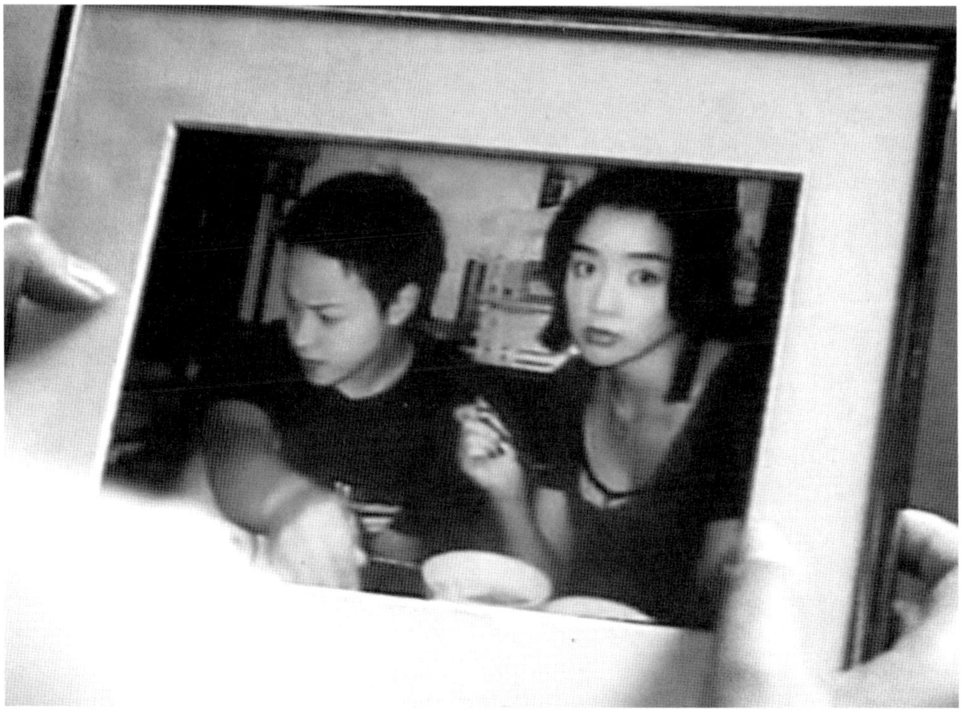
◀ 73

74 ▼

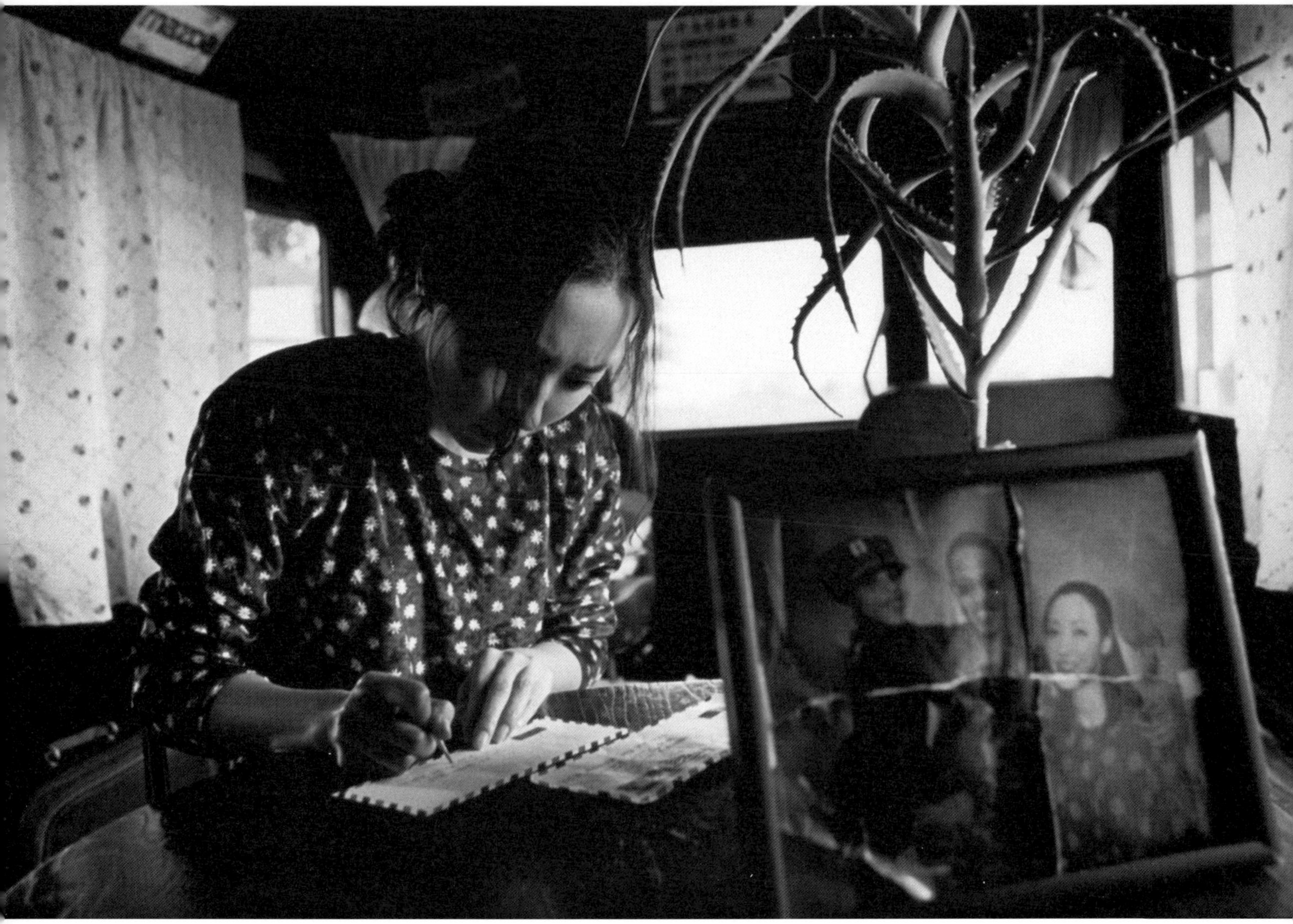

▼ 75

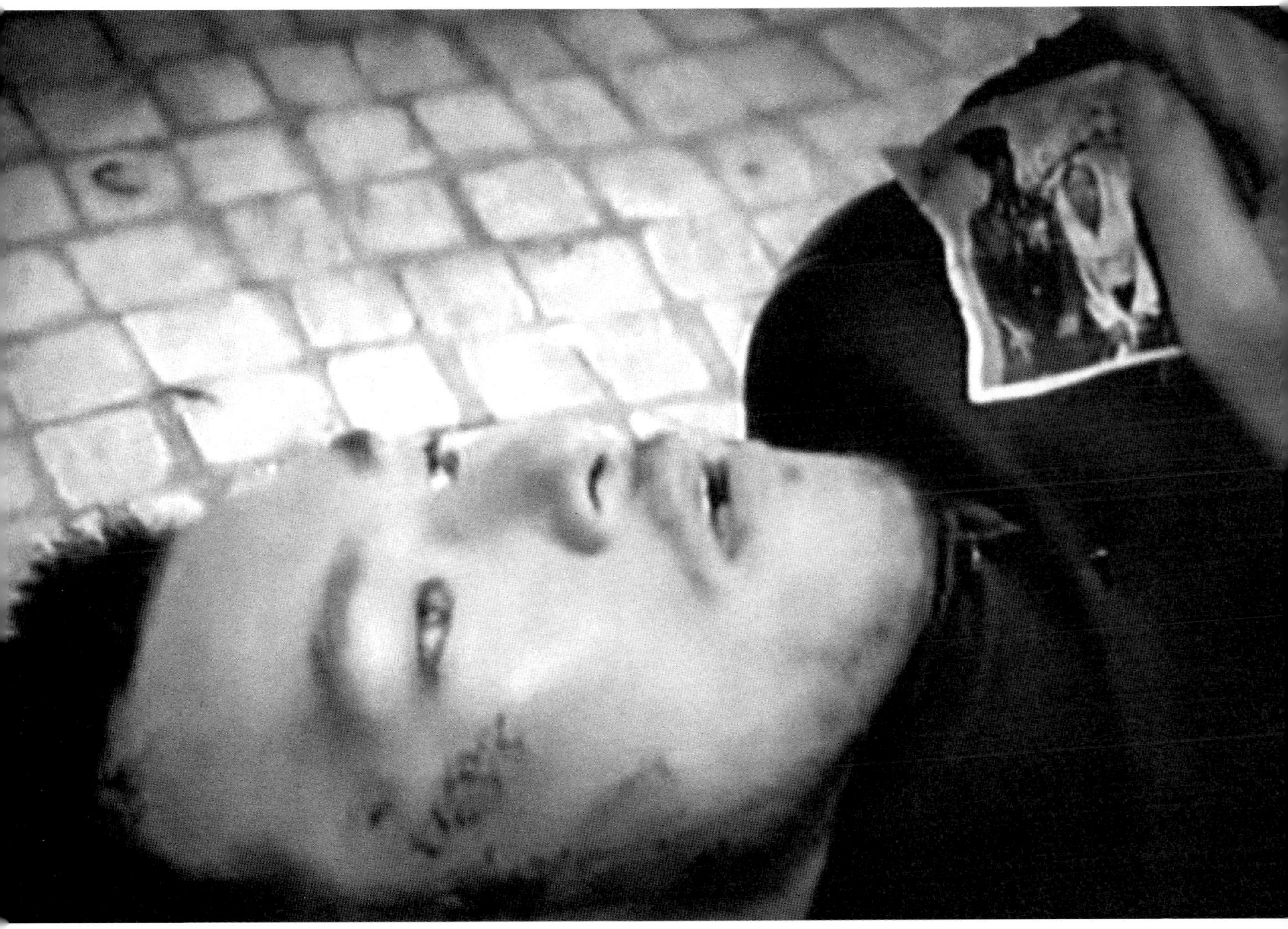

76 ▶

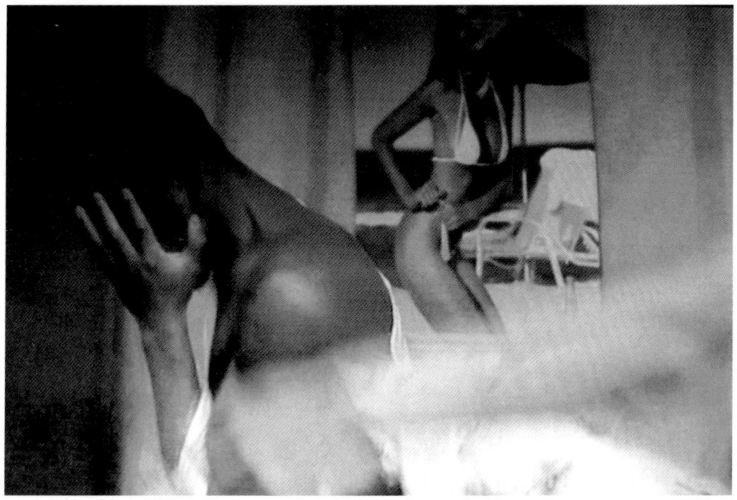

77 ▶

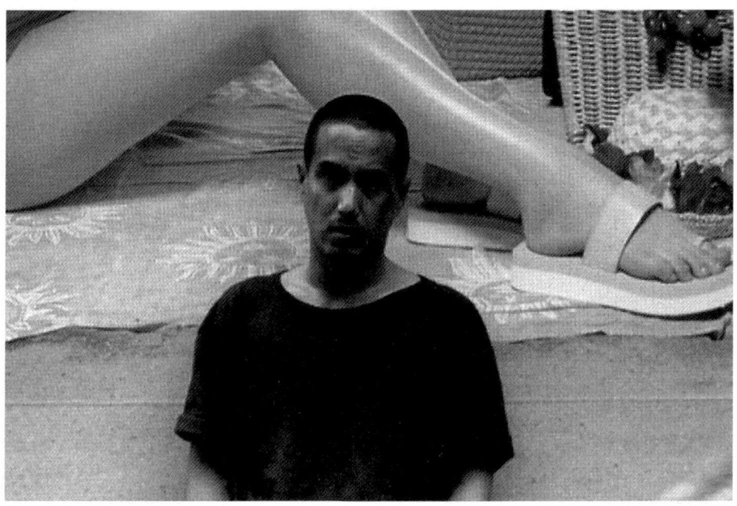

BLACK AND WHITE ARE THE SAME COLOR

This interview* by e-mail has been made with a series of questions sent to Kim Ki-duk on the 5th September 2005. Kim Ki-duk's answers are dated the 6th September 2005.

**Translated into French from Korean by Young-Sook Kim*

What are your sources of inspiration for the themes you tackle in your films: the street, the media, your own experiences?

I've had various experiences. In Korea, for family reasons, I couldn't carry on studying like everyone else. As soon as I was 16 I worked in a factory for 6 years. Then I enrolled in the Marines.
In the factory I handled many machines and learned a lot about their functioning which is, I think, quite similar to that of human life in the sense that the machine uses opposite forces, playing on their balance to create a product.
My various experiences, life in the Marines, religious studies and my experience as a painter have brought me the fundamental images of my cinematic practice. Like the world, at the same time very simple and very complex, everything can appear different or identical depending on our perception. For example, religion, mathematics, science and philosophy are for me one and the same thing. Mathematics are exact, science is full of hazards, philosophy is ambiguous and religion mysterious. But it all has the same meaning. And that is also valid for my films. For me, black and white are the same colour, facing each other. The world is born and dies in their conflict. So we must live in balance between the black and white which are in us.
That is what I try to express in my cinema. I don't speak as a philosopher or theologian, but from what I draw from my experience of life.

What role do morals play in your reflection on our "civilized" societies?

In Korea, we are taught morals from childhood. That provokes a lot of problems in adolescence. In case of moral failure, it is despair and tormented conscience. Those who fail on the moral level are humiliated, people turn away from them. That is the method of civilized society.
Inner disposition, upbringing and society contribute to build the personality. But, as those elements diverge, it is very difficult to conform to an established order. My films talk about those conflicts. But rather than give great importance to morals, I'm trying to get to know human nature in depth.
In my opinion, all the answers are to be found in nature. In water. In a tree. Even in a stone. I am not a Buddhist and I haven't studied Buddhism.
Spring, Summer… for example, is not a film on Buddhism but a film on the time lived by the man, a story on the tree, a story on the water, a story on nature.
That film tells us that man belongs to nature too.

What meaning do you give to the fish, a recurrent figure in your films?

In my films, various living beings, man and nature, are treated on the same level. All those living beings express the character and action of man.
We keep in mind too many images already seen elsewhere, in music, painting and films, and we look through them too much. I am not interested in that.
In my films, living beings, natural landscapes and objects are all as important as the actors.

What relationships or functions do places have in the structure of your narratives?

I artificially create cinematographic places to situate characters in them and tell a story of

my choice. What I want to show is that such a story can happen in any place but that, wherever it happens, our life has its fill of difficulties.
So, I shoot in a certain place and try to show life inside that framework.

What relationships do the places have with the characters?

My characters don't represent individual people but several aspects which are in us. So a character in my film is at the same time nobody and all of us. I even think that they are at the same time both people who approve of my film and people who disapprove.

What are your criteria for choosing to shoot in a studio or in natural settings?

I almost never shoot in a studio. I might shoot, for example, in a very tiny house and I can thus employ very little material for the shooting and the lighting because of the smallness of the place. I look for places which correspond best to the scenario to shoot the film in its entirety. However, I think one can always change places. Like human beings can live anywhere in the world, I don't give too much importance to a particular place.

What does the script stage represent in your cinematographic work?

I first write the most realistic script possible. I also write the dialogues. At the moment of rewriting, I modify it gradually to move it towards abstraction. When the feel is right, I also reduce the dialogues. It's a bit like making first a realistic sculpture of a human being, then finally reworking it by cutting it into facets. During those stages a story and images merge together. In the end I obtain a "semi-abstract" film.

"Semi-abstract", what does that mean? Does it depend on other strategies of representation?

"Semi-abstract" means the junction between reality and the imaginary. Even though reality is hard to live, we can perceive it differently. It's like the "semi-abstract" in sculpture. *3-iron* illustrates that very well. If black represents reality, white represents the imaginary. In a word, it's the same thing.

For your research in narratives, do you draw from other cinemas?

I find ideas for my films not in films but in social news items. Western cinema critics notice the influence of great Western directors on Asian directors, but that's not my case. I often watch people, that helps me a lot to find cinematographic ideas. I don't have ideas fixed in advance. I come across an idea for a film by chance, when observing people, society, nature. And I create a story. I do appreciate the works of other people, whether a book or a film, but copying them doesn't interest me. I want to express myself with my own energy.

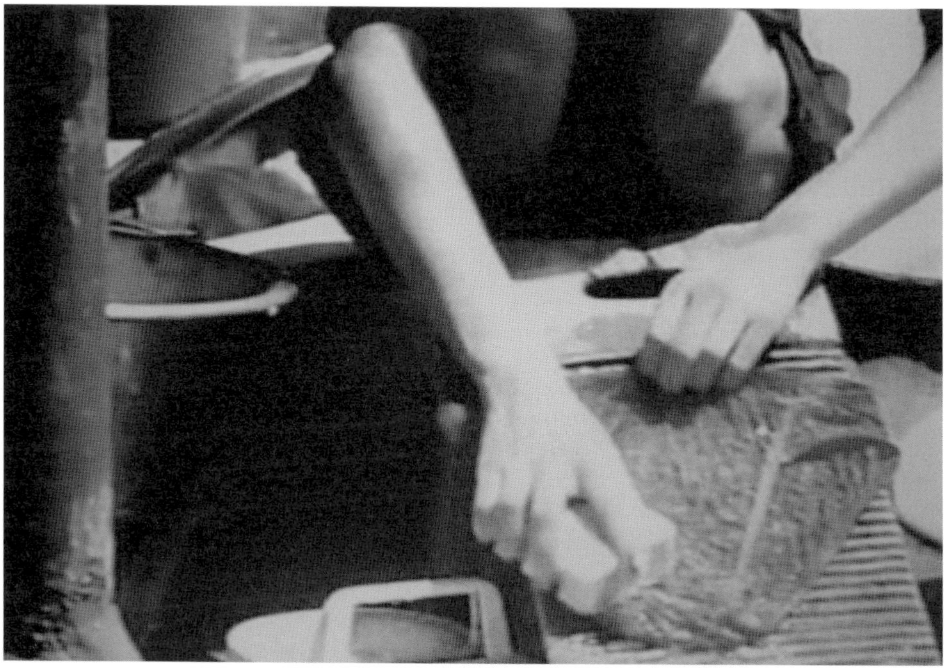

◄ 78

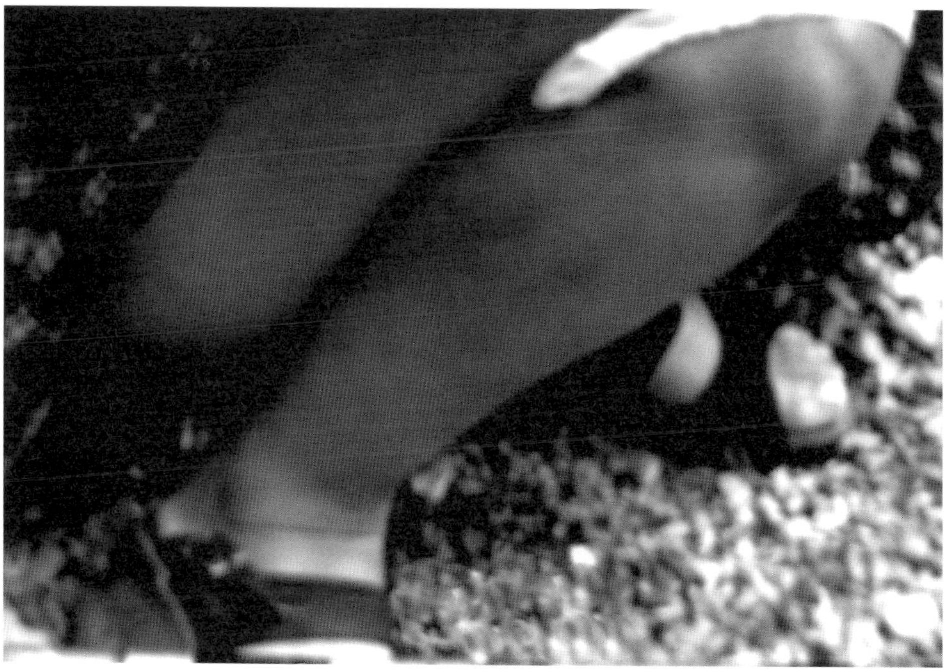

◄ 79

Can we say that your work as a film director is based on an aesthetics of cruelty?

In my opinion, it is not my films which are cruel, but contemporary life. The news on CNN is much more shocking and cruel than my films.

Do you think about the actors already when writing the script?

No.

What is the influence of the actor's personality on your films?

Whatever actor is found in my film, that's the destiny of my film. I don't sack an actor because he/she plays badly. I finish the shoot with them, whatever happens.

Does the use of recurrent characters with changing identities and interpersonal relationships between characters form as many autobiographical facets for you?

They are all the people I've met and who've touched me.

The relationship to the body occupies a very important place in your work… For lack of dialogues, do you try to describe the movements, like choreographers do?

Men's actions, physiological functions, are all expressions. I think that acts are more reliable than spoken words.

The main male characters in your films give the impression of existing only in excess and chaos. In what can that inner conflict between reason and the tangible serve as a motor for existing?

As a human being I wanted to have various experience. We live the infinite repetition of nights and days. Our life oscillates between plus and minus. We live in the confrontation of opposites. In my opinion, the ideal would be to alternate between that "plus" and that "minus". I believe the characters in my films possess that energy.

Women also have an important place, not only through their presence as characters, but through your art references: Egon Schiele, Camille Claudel… Contrary to some criticisms that have been made about you, couldn't we say that your cinema ties in with feminist cinema?

I make films on the principle which rules humanity and nature. But I don't think all critics realize that or understand that. Thanks to women I live with 50% more energy. They are half of my life. If women represent white, I represent black, but it is the same colour of human being. Despite that, I think that women are more mysterious than men.

Do you go on looking for locations during the writing of the script?

Yes.

Is the script finished when you start shooting?

I shoot while modifying it.

Do you film in the order of the script?

I try to do so.

What improvisational role is left to the camera, to the actors?

I allow the actors to do what they want during shooting. When I edit, I re-think to see if I keep it.

How do you choose the actors?

I work with beginners as much as possible. The audience has preconceived ideas with well-known actors.

Do you do the casting yourself?

It is done by the assistant director but I make the final decisions.

The titles of your films are very laconic. A bit like titles of paintings. How do you choose them?

I decide, according to the feeling. I try to choose a Korean title if possible.

In Wild Animals, *during an argument with a painter on questions of aesthetics, the character played by Cho Jae-Hyun adds blood to the painter's canvas. Is it a metaphor for your passage from painting to cinema?*

It's possible, but I don't know any more. What is certain is that my films are the continuation of my work as a painter.

Is the silence that characterizes your characters a survival of the silence of the painting?

I don't know. It seems to me that as I grow older, I understand that spoken words don't have much importance.

When you returned to Korea after your stay in Europe, what was the meeting – or the occasion – at the origin of those new experiences which made you abandon painting to write your first scripts?

I felt like doing something else. Before I die, I want to do lots of things. I want to try to make sculpture too.

You came back to Korea in 1994. In 1993, a new president had just been elected. Did that political change have an influence on your decision to return to Korea?

No. I was not interested in politics. I love Korea. I especially love nature in Korea.
(...) I am a director who makes films. I don't like to talk and I've responded the best I can to the questions in this interview. My answer to all questions is this, and this alone: "Black and white are the same colour."

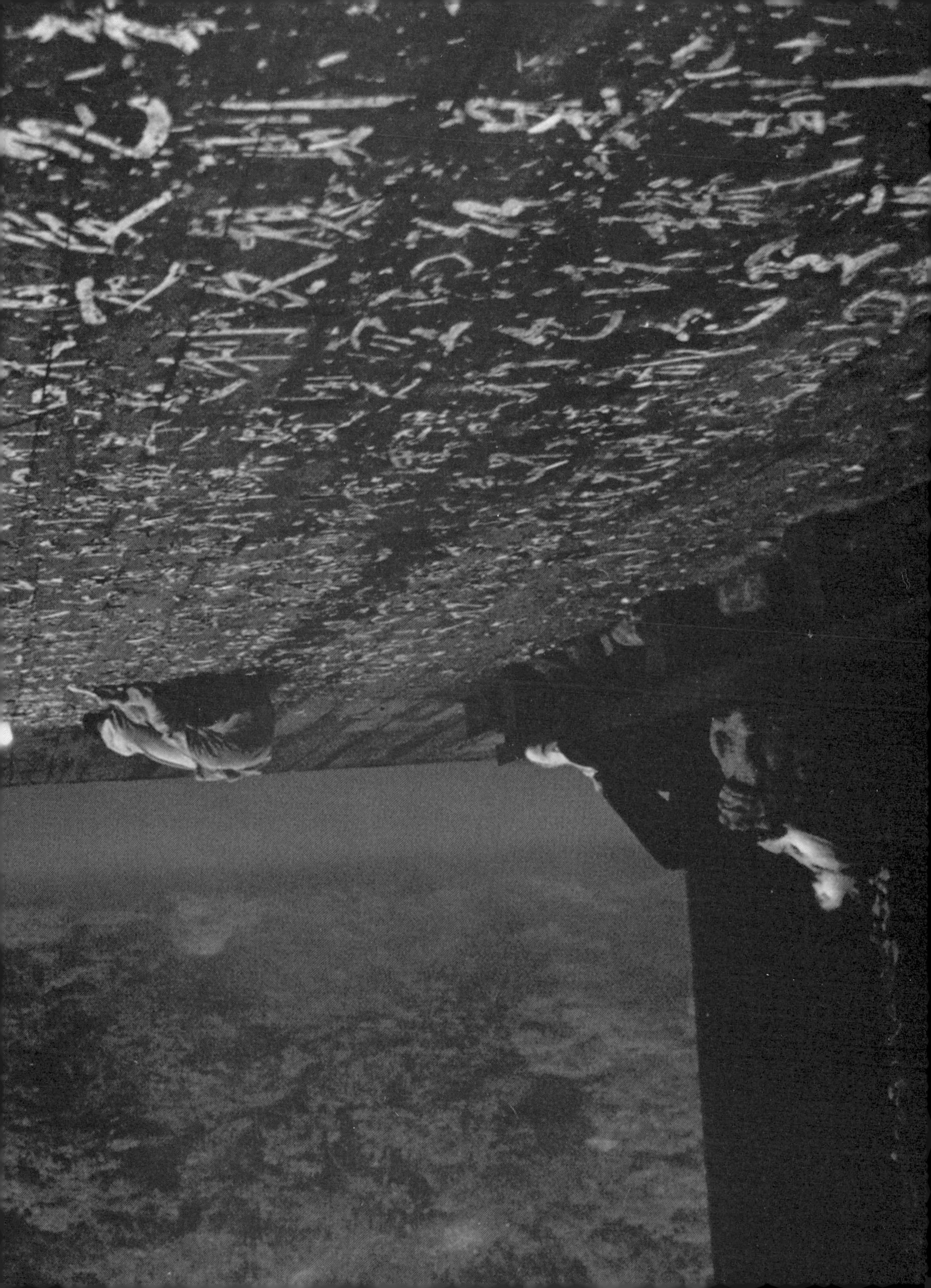

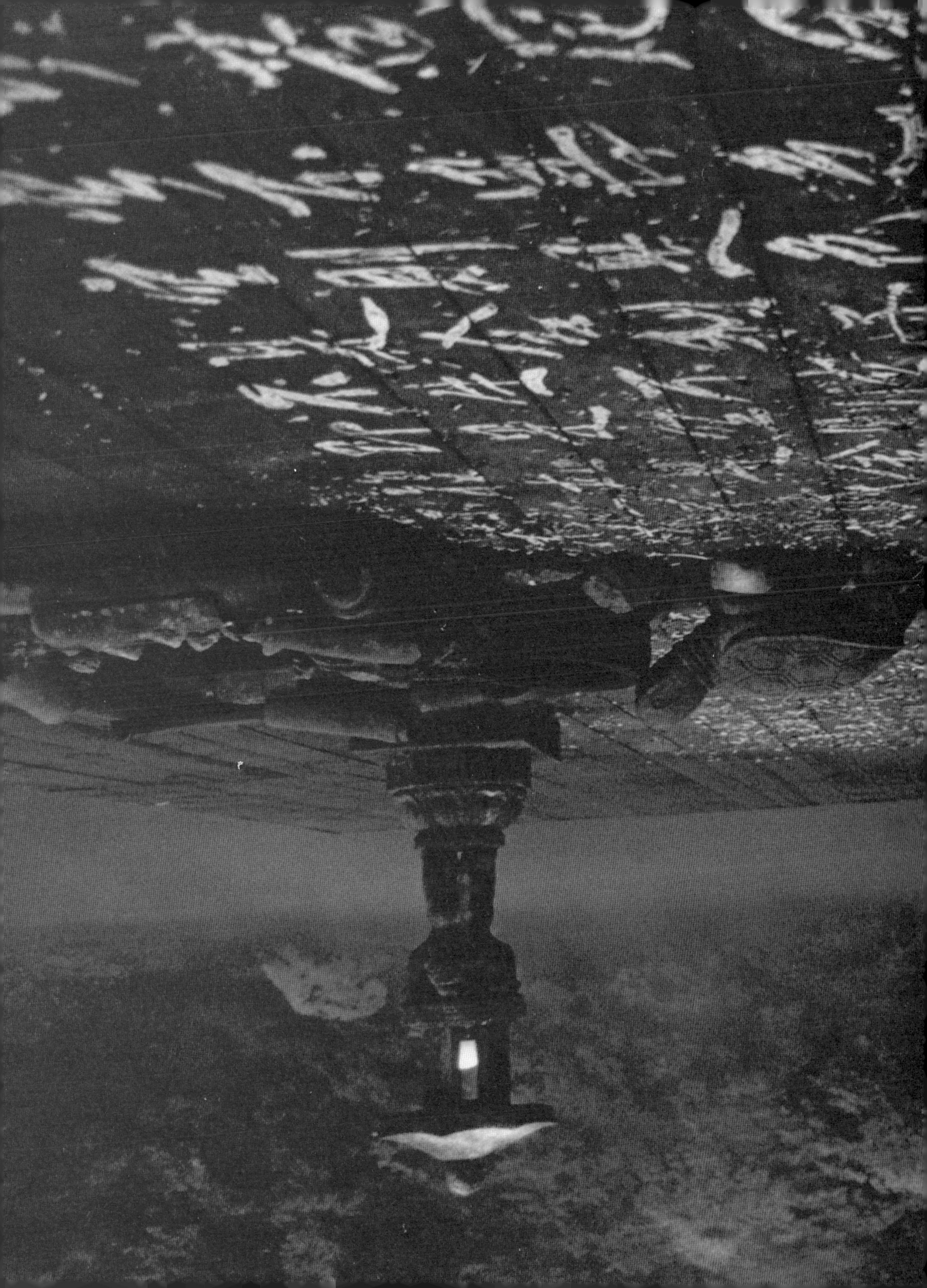

BIOGRAPHY

80 ▲

Kim Ki-duk was born in 1960 in Bonghwa, a village in the mountains of the Kyungsang province in South Korea. He left at nine to settle with his family on the outskirts of Seoul.

His elder brother expelled from school, he was forced by his father to abandon school and attend an agricultural college. At sixteen he worked in various factories, then enrolled six years later in the Marines to do his military service. At twenty-eight, free from his military obligations, and not knowing what to do he lived in a church – in exchange for some voluntary work – welcoming blind people. He contemplated becoming a priest, then finally decided to consecrate himself to painting.

In 1990, gathering all his savings, he left Korea to travel across Europe (from Finland to Greece, via Germany). In 1992, after a stay in Paris, he settled in a village near Montpellier in the South of France. He sold a few paintings in order to survive and discovered cinema.

Returning to Korea three years later, he pursued a course in script writing, wrote his first scenario and won numerous prizes, including that for Best Korean Script Writer with *Painter and Prisoner*. Then he won another prize from the Korean Motion Picture Association with his second script, *Illegal Crossing*. The following year, Kim Ki-duk finally had the chance to write and shoot his first film. With no experience whatsoever, he made his cinematic debut with *Crocodile*, shooting from his next script. Since then, he has written all his own scripts.

Today Kim Ki-duk is counted among the most talented directors of the new generation of Korean directors. With his very first films he acquired more of a reputation in the West, mainly through international festivals like those in Berlin, Locarno and Venice, than in his own country, where he encountered the wrath of feminists and is the subject of controversies. Despite growing success Kim Ki-duk maintains his own way of working in order to keep his independence: small budget, fast shooting and strong personal implications which make him create his own backgrounds and accessories.

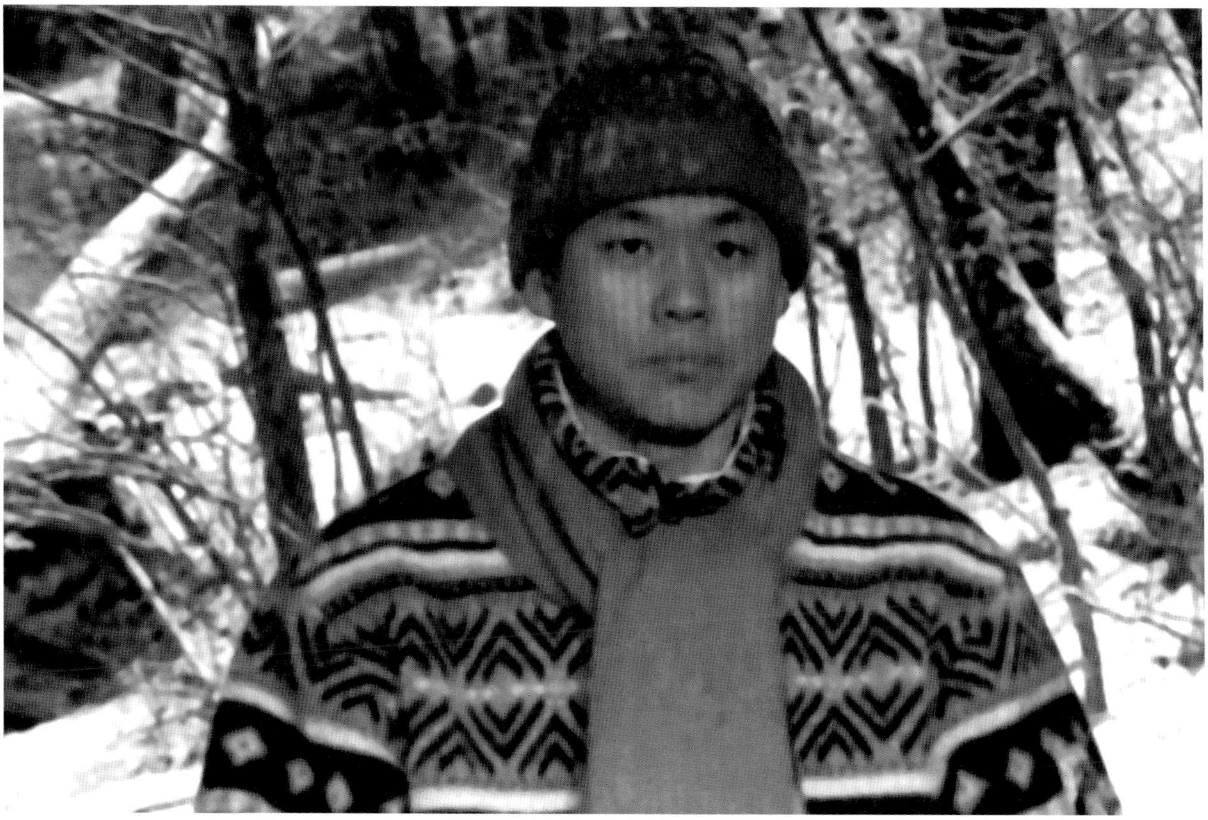

◀ 81

82 ▼

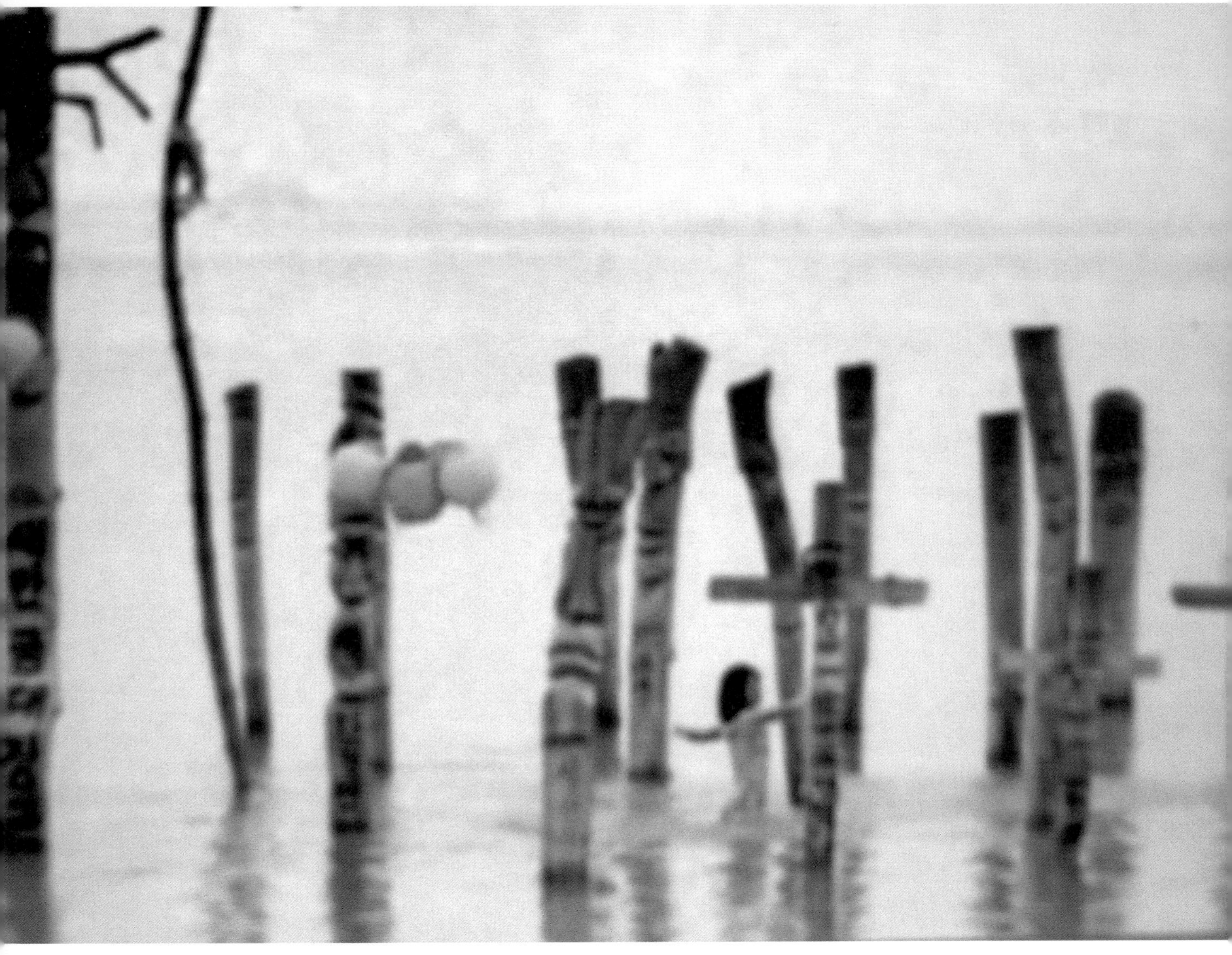

FILMOGRAPHY

Script

1994 PAINTER AND PRISONIER
1995 ILLEGAL CROSSING

Script & Direction

1996 CROCODILE (*Alligator-Ag-O*)
color - 35mm- 102'

Cast: Ahn Jae-Hong, Cho Jae-Hyon, Woo Yun-Kyeong, Jeon Mu-Song.
Screenplay: Kim Ki-duk
Producer: Kim Byung-Su
Production: Joninbang
Music: Yi Mun-Hee
Cinematography: Dong-sam Lee
Editor: Gok-ji Park

1997 WILD ANIMALS (*Yaesaeng tongmul p'oho kuyok*)
color - 35mm - 105'

Cast: Jang Dong-Jik, Cho Jae-Hyun, Denis Lavant, Joh Jae-hyun, Ryun Jang, Sasha Rucavina, Cho Jae-Hyung, Jang Dong-Jik, Richard Bohringer, Laurent Buro
Screenplay: Kim Ki-duk
Producer: Kwon Ki-yung
Production: Dreamcinema
Music: Kang In-gu, Oh Jin-ha
Cinematography: Suh Jong-min
Editor: Park Suhn-duk
Set Designer, Art Direction:
Kim Ki-duk

1998 BIRDCAGE INN (*Paran Daemun*)
color - 35mm - 105'

Cast: Ji-eun Lee - Hae-eun Lee - Jae-mo Ahn - Hyeong-gi Jeong - Min-seok
Screenplay: Kim Ki-duk
Producer: Seung-jae Lee
Music: Moon-Hui Lee
Cinematography: Jeong-min Seo
Editor: Im-Pyo Ko

Awards from: Paran daemun (1998) AFI Fest (1999)

2000 THE ISLE (*Seom*)
color - 35mm - 105'

Cast: Jung Suh, Yoosuk Kim, Sung-hee Park, Jae-hyeon Jo, Hang-Seon Jang, Yeo-jin Kim, Won Seo
Screenplay: Kim Ki-duk
Producer: Eun Lee
Production: Myung Films Production
Music: Sang-yun Jeon
Cinematography: Seo-shik Hwang
Editor: Kyung Min-Ho
Set Designer: Kim Ki-duk

Awards from: Seom (2000) Venice Film Festival (2000) Brussels International Festival of Fantasy Film (2001)

2000 REAL FICTION (*Silje Sanghwang*)
color - 35mm - 103'

Cast: Ju Jin-mo, Kim Jin-ah, Son Min-suk, Lee Je-rak, Kim Ki-yun, Myeong Sun-mi, Hyeong-seong Jang
Screenplay: Kim Ki-duk
Producer: Harry Lee, Shin Sung-Su
Production: Shin Sung-Su Production
Music: Sang-yun Jeon
Cinematography: Hwang Chul-hyun
Editor: Kyung Min-ho
Set Designer: Kim Ki-duk

Awards from: Shilje sanghwang (2000) - Moscow International Film Festival (2001)

2001 ADDRESS UNKNOWN (*Soochwieen bodmyung*)
color - 35mm - 117'

Cast: Dong-kun Yang, Min-jung Ban, Young-min Kim, Eun-jin Bang, Gye-nam Myeong, In-ok Lee, Jae-hyeon Jo
Screenplay: Kim Ki-duk
Producer: Seung-jae Lee
Music: Ho-jun Park
Cinematography: Jeong-min Seo
Editor: Sung-won Ham
Set Designer, Art Direction:
Kim Ki-duk

Awards from: Venice Film Festival (2001) - Grand Bell Awards, South Korea (2002)

2001 BAD GUY (*Na-Bbun-Nam-Ja*)
color - 35mm - 100'

Cast: Jae-hyeon Jo, Won Seo, Yun-tae Kim, Duek-mun Choi, Yoon-young Choi, Yoo-jin Shin, Jung-young Kim, Gung-Min Nam
Screenplay: Kim Ki-Duk
Producer: Lee Seung-Jai
Production: E Tube Entertainment/CJ Entertainment/Light&Joy Film
Music: Park Ho-Jun
Cinematography: Hwang Choi-Hyun
Editor: Seong-won Hang

Awards from: Nabbeun namja (2001) - Berlin International Film Festival (2002)

2002 COASTGUARD (*Hae anseon*)
color - 35mm - 91'

Cast: Dong-Kun Jang, Jeong-hak Kim, Ji-a Park, Hye-jin Yu, Jin Jeong, Gu-taek Kim, Kang-woo Kim, Yun-jae Park, Tae-woo Kim, Yeong-jae Kim
Screenplay: Kim Ki-duk
Producer: Seung-jae Lee
Music: Jang Young-gyu
Cinematography: Dong-hyeon Baek
Editor: Seon Min Kim
Art Direction: Ju-hun Yun

Awards from: Karlovy Vary International Film Festival (2003)

2003 SPRING, SUMMER, FALL, WINTER... AND SPRING
(Bom yeoreum gaeul gyeoul geurigo bom)
color - 35mm - 103'

Cast: Yeong-su Oh, Ki-duk Kim, Young-min Kim, Jae-kyeong Seo, Yeo-jin Ha, Jong-ho Kim, Jung-young Kim, Dae-han Ji, Min Choi, Ji-a Park, Min-Young Song
Screenplay: Kim Ki-Duk
Producer: Karl Baumgartner, Lee Seung-Jae
Production: Pandora Film, U.S.A.
Music: Ji-woong Park
Cinematography: Dong-hyeon Baek
Editor: Kim Ki-duk
Costume Designer: Kim Min-Hee

Awards from: Locarno International Film Festival (2003) - San Sebastián International Film Festival (2003) - European Film Awards (2003) - Blue Dragon Awards (2003) - Golden Satellite Awards (2004) - Bangkok International Film Festival (2004) - Argentinean Film Critics Association (2005)

2004 SAMARITAN GIRL
color - 35mm - 95'

Cast: Yeo-reum Han, Ji-min Kwak, Eol Lee, Kwon Hyun-Min, Oh Young, Im Gyun-Ho, Lee Jong-Gil, Shin Taek-Ki, Jung-gi Park, Gul-seon Kim, Seung-won Seo, Yoo Jae-Ik, Jung In-Gi, Jin-bae Jeon, Yook Sae-Jin
Screenplay: Kim Ki-Duk
Producer: Jeong-min Baek
Executive Producer : Kim Ki-Duk, Kim Yoon-ho
Music: Park Ji & Ji-Woong Park
Cinematography: Sun Sang-Jae, Sang-jae Seon
Editor: Kim Ki-duk
Art Direction: Kim Ki-duk

Awards from: Berlin International Film Festival (2004)

2005 3-IRON (*Bin-jip*)
color - 35mm - 88'

Cast: Seung-yeon Lee, Hyun-kyoon Lee, Hyuk-ho Kwon, Jin-mo Ju, Jeong-ho Choi, Ju-seok Lee, Mi-suk Lee, Sung-hyuk Moon, Jee-ah Park, Jae-yong Jang, Dah-hae Lee
Screenplay: Kim Ki-duk
Producer: Kim Ki-duk
Music: Slvian
Song: Natacha Atlas
Cinematography: Seong-back Jang
Editor: Kim Ki-duk
Art Direction: Kim Hyun-joo

Awards from: European Film Awards (2004) - David di Donatello Awards (2005) - Italian National Syndicate of Film Journalists 2005 -San Sebastián International Film Festival (2005) - Valladolid International Film Festival (2004) - Venice Film Festival (2004)

2005 THE BOW (*Hwal*)
color - 35mm - 90'

Cast: Yeo-reum Han, Si-jeok Seo, Gook-hwan Jeon, Seong-hwang Jeon
Screenplay: Kim Ki-duk
Producer: Kim Ki-duk
Production: Seok-bin Jang
Music: Eun-il Kang
Cinematography: Seong-back Jang
Editor: Kim Ki-duk
Art Direction: Sol Art Chung

Film premieres in "Un Certain Regard" —Cannes Film Festival 2005

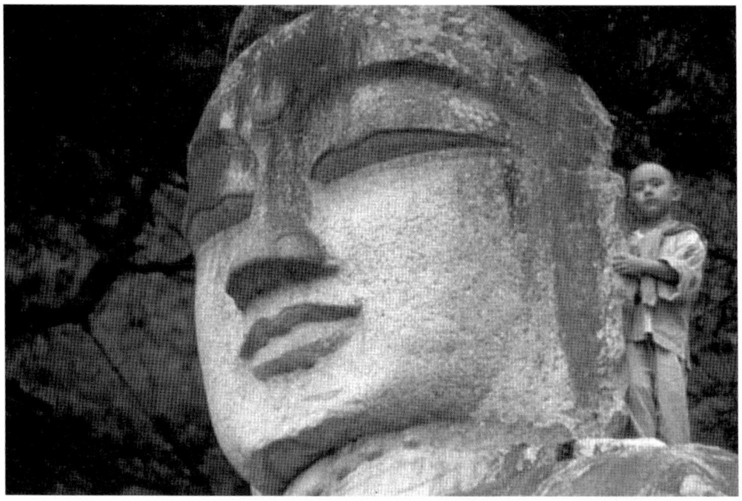
◀ 83

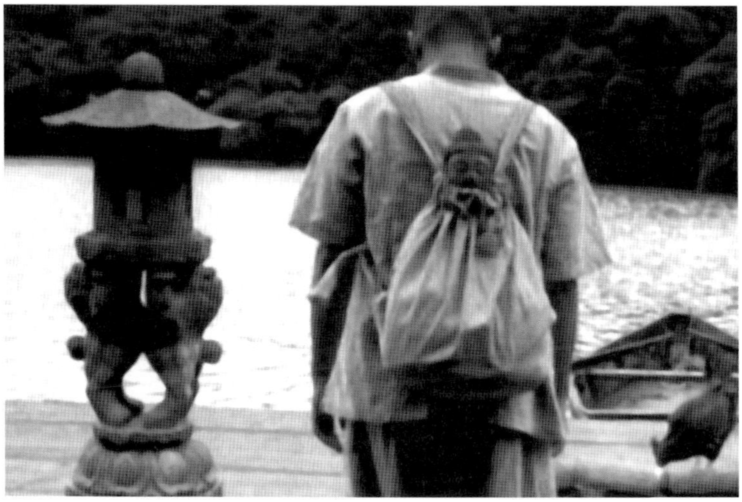
◀ 84

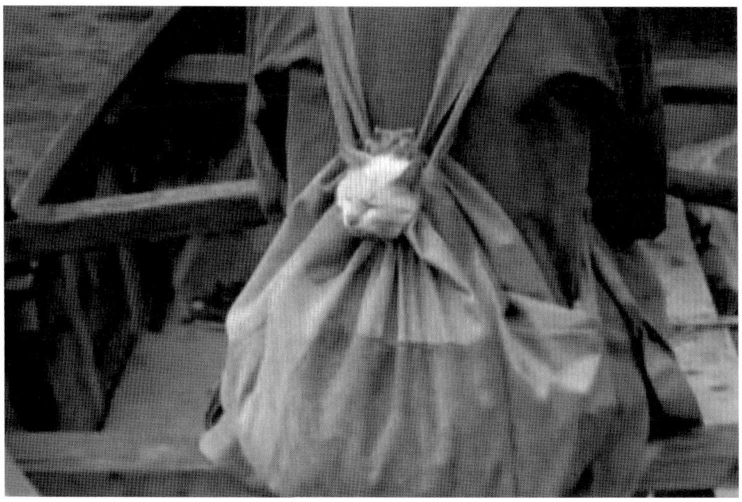
◀ 85

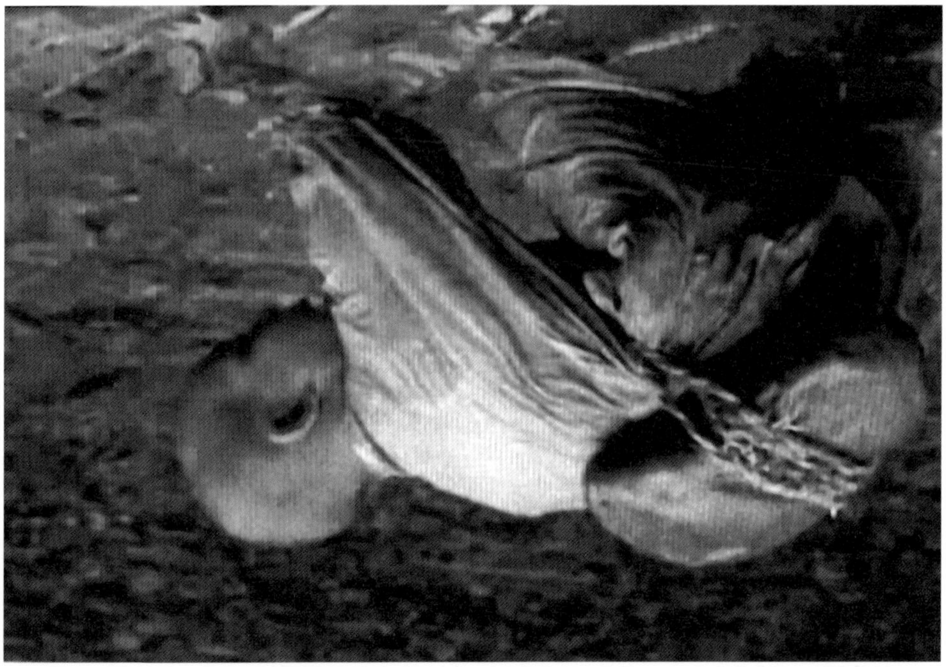

◄ 98

PHOTO INDEX

87 ▶

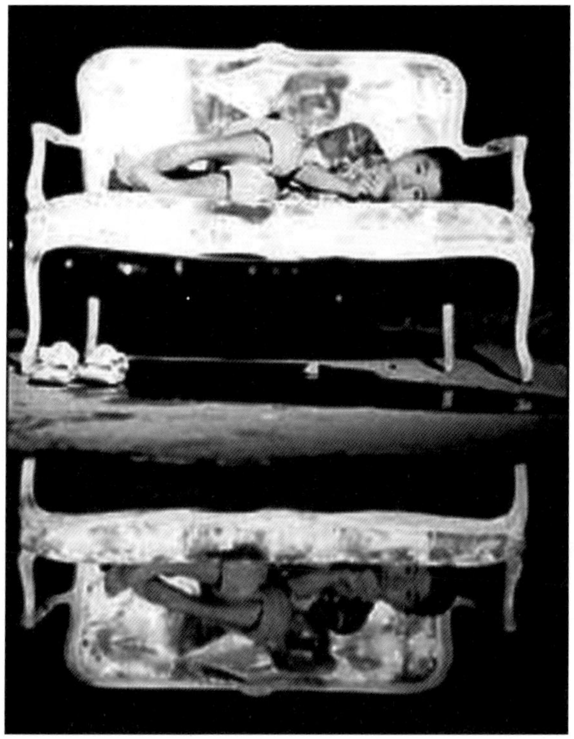

Printed by
POLICROM
Barcelona - Spain
Spring 2006